"I am extremely impressed with *Fashioned by Faith*. Rachel has done an outstanding job relating to young girls while proving her points with strong Bible references and verses. I work with young ladies every day at my dance studio, and it is amazing what they will say or wear without a second thought. I have already encouraged my dancers to get a copy of this book. I am proud to say that Rachel did it—a positive spin on fashion from a model who is a Christian. Hallelujah!"

—Tammy Johns, Mrs. United States 2009

"In her new book, *Fashioned by Faith*, Rachel Lee Carter has beautifully blended elements of purity and loveliness without condescending attitudes or impossible expectations. God's Word for women and girls of all ages stands the test of time, and this book proves that once and for all."

—Eva Marie Everson and Jessica Everson, Authors of *Sex, Lies, and the Media* and *Sex, Lies, and High School*

"It was evident to me from the first time we met, that Rachel had a deep spiritual core. As a makeup artist in the fashion industry, it has been a pleasure working with someone whose inner light and beauty touches those around her. *Fashioned by Faith* will be a blessing to all who read it."

—Maria Buchanan, Professional Print and Commercial Makeup Artist

"It's not everyday that you find modesty in the fashion industry but somehow Rachel pulls it off in her career and in her book, *Fashioned by Faith*. Modesty seems to be a lost virtue in most homes and churches today and most girls don't realize that a real and godly man looks for that virtue in a future spouse. It's refreshing to know there are roll models still in this business for young women to look up to and aspire to be like."

—**Bradley Tharington,** Professional Male Model, 15+ years

"As a youth pastor and father of two daughters, I am well acquainted with how the current culture has corrupted our view of beauty. I am excited about this book and what it will do to change the way young ladies think about how they dress. Rachel has drawn on her years of experience in the modeling industry and her biblical training at Word of Life to address this subject in a fresh new way. I highly recommend this book to young ladies, parents and student groups. It is a must read!"

—**David Mills,** Youth Pastor

"In *Fashioned by Faith*, Rachel shares her experience, struggles and real-world issues. Readers will be able to associate with many of them. Yet it is evident that her strong faith in God has strengthened and sustained her throughout her modeling career and life. I have had the great pleasure to know and model with Rachel for over 20 years. Her love for God radiates to everyone she meets."

—**Sabrina Nosal-Ward,** Professional Plus-size Model, 25+ yrs.

"We desperately need to share God's vision on modesty to our young ladies' and this book is the perfect tool to use along with your Bible to get them engaged in conversation and personal discovery in God's Word."

—**Meg Wylie,** Art Director of Photography

FASHIONED by FAITH

FASHI(by)ONED
FAITH

RACHEL LEE CARTER

THOMAS NELSON
Since 1798

NASHVILLE   DALLAS   MEXICO CITY   RIO DE JANEIRO

Published in Nashville, Tennessee, by Thomas Nelson. Thomas Nelson is a registered trademark of Thomas Nelson, Inc.

Fashioned by Faith is represented by Les Stobbe of the Leslie H. Stobbe Literary Agency, lhstobbe123@gmail.com

Cover photos by Shane Greene
Makeup by Julie Abernathy
All unmarked photos used with permission of author, Rachel Lee Carter

Thomas Nelson, Inc., titles may be purchased in bulk for educational, business, fund-raising, or sales promotional use. For information, please e-mail SpecialMarkets@ThomasNelson.com.

Library of Congress Cataloging-in-Publication Data
An application for Cataloging-in-Publication Data has been filed.

ISBN 978-1-4003-1692-2

CPSIA:
Mfr: RR Donnelley/Crawfordsville, IN/February, 2011—PPO# 117812

For my three boys: Daryl, Jack, and Jude

Contents

Foreword

"If you've got it, flaunt it." "Look steamy in your bikini!" "476 ways to look sexy for spring!" We've heard it all. As women and young girls, we are bombarded with messages like these from advertisers, the media, and the fashion and entertainment industries.

As a professional model, commercial actress for more than twenty-five years, and a former beauty queen, I listened to those messages for longer than I'd like to admit. You could say I've been there, done that, and got the tight T-shirt. But thanks be to God, I gave my life to Christ in 1999, and I invited Him not only into my heart, my life, and my family, but yes, even into my closet! And when I did that, I realized that God had a lot to say about how we women present ourselves . . . how our bodies are temples of the Holy Spirit and how we should glorify God with our bodies. God knew that we would be fighting this battle in our present day and time, and he is raising up powerful women like Rachel to remind us of God's eternal truths about women, our sexuality, our femininity, and how to remain true to our Christian convictions while still dressing in the latest styles.

Rachel does a fantastic job of delving into God's Word and helping us see these topics explored from a Christian perspective. She not only shares with the reader what God thinks about beauty, modesty, and our femininity, but she also shares her real-life experiences of working as a professional model for the last twenty years and the challenges of living these virtues.

Women want to feel attractive. Having grown up in the fashion industry myself and working alongside Rachel on modeling jobs, I know and understand the pressures that girls feel every day. But revealing our bodies and putting too much emphasis on looking "hot and sexy" is not the answer to our search for happiness. The over-sexualization of our culture has not made us happier as girls and women. Teen girls have higher rates of depression, suicide, and STDs than ever before. Families are crumbling around us, the media has become more and more crude, and the plague of pornography addiction continues to spread around the world. It's time we go back to living the way God asked us to.

God's way is always the best way. Enjoy this book and take the advice and learn to live it. It will bless you, your friends, and men all around you . . . young and old. And with women working together, I truly believe that we can begin to change our culture . . . one outfit at a time!

May God bless you!

—Brenda Sharman
Founding National Director of the
International Pure Fashion Program and
National Spokesperson for Pure Fashion
(www.purefashion.com)

Don't let anyone look down on you because you are young, but set an example for the believers, in speech, in life, in love, in faith and in purity.

—1 Timothy 4:12

Dear Friend,

I'm excited about what's in store for you as you delve into the topic of modesty, but first I want to take some time to tell you about myself and what you can expect from the following pages. I've been a professional model for twenty-plus years, and by now I'm a bona fide clothes fanatic. I've modeled for some of the biggest names in the industry. Among them are some I'm sure you've heard of, like CoverGirl, Tommy Hilfiger, Reebok, and hundreds, possibly thousands more. My experience as a model provides me with a unique perspective, and now I want to pass this perspective on to you.

As you read, you'll be introduced to the seductive world of high fashion, and I'll share with you the positive and negative impact it's had on my life. I'll use stories from my career traveling the globe to give you new insight into the controversial subject matter of modesty. We will also hear what guys have to say about it, what I've learned about it, and of course, what God's Word teaches about it. At the end of each chapter, you will find some follow-up questions that you can use to dig a little deeper into the issues and ideas we have covered. For a more in-depth look at what God has to say about modesty, I have created a nine-week study in the back of the book. You can go through this study by yourself in your daily quiet times, or with a group of friends. My prayer is that through both of these tools, you will grow closer to God as you deepen your relationship with Him through His Word.

Modeling hasn't just been my job; it's been my life, and from it came my deep love for fashion. Likewise, with my faith comes my deep love for the Lord. Years ago, I set out to discover if the two could coexist in my heart without conflict. At a time when the most popular catchphrase from the advertising world is "Sex sells," is there a way to wear the latest fashions without dishonoring God and His will for my life? I needed to know, and now I want to share my discoveries with you. Let me be your guide as we embark on this journey to uncover the truth about modesty and what it means to be fashioned by FAITH!

Love, Rachel

Chapter One

Fashioned by Freedom!

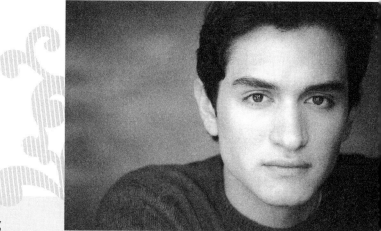

Photo by Natalie Young

Seth

Age: 20
State: California
Interests: acting, painting, photography,
travel, Spanish culture, art
Future ambition: actor

he says . . .

I grew up with two older sisters. They've taught me a lot about
women. One of the things I've learned is there is a quiet and beautiful dignity about a woman who dresses conservatively. Any man

would be fortunate to have a wife like my sisters, but what makes them really special is that they have too much self-respect and confidence to wear clothes that reveal too much. I use the word *confidence* because I feel a girl who's covered in all the right places is a girl who lives with the freedom of not having to rely on attention for her sense of self-worth. A girl with confidence is much more attractive to me than a girl who feels she has to exploit her body to receive attention or, worse, love.

My sisters are not ashamed of their bodies, and they wear the most current and stylish clothes. Yet they understand great men appreciate modesty. It doesn't matter how many girlfriends a man has had in his past, when he decides to settle down, his ideal wife will be one who lives modestly. A man who says he doesn't care about modesty or how his girlfriend dresses is lying.

When I marry, I want to find a woman I alone can fully appreciate. I believe young women should learn to value a sense of mystery. The more a woman destroys the mystery for a man, the more he will only be interested in what's going on from the neck down. All men are guilty of it, including myself, unfortunately. When a girl can barely walk because of her tight-fitting or revealing clothes, a man will either pursue her solely out of lust or automatically dismiss her as someone he doesn't want to be with.

There's a saying that goes, "If you've got it, flaunt it." This is a lie. Instead, it should say, "If you've got it, protect it." Great women like my mother and sisters took this idea and lived their lives by it. This is the type of woman I'm interested in getting to know, because modesty and confidence in a woman is a very powerful and attractive combination.

—Seth

she says . . .

As a professional model of more than twenty years, I've been blessed to travel the world and work for some of the biggest names in the business. I've dined next to the king of Spain's mansion and sailed on the *Aladdin*, the king of Jordan's yacht. I've experienced temperatures from 114 degrees Fahrenheit to 44 below zero. I've eaten unique cuisine, from brains and ostrich to kangaroo and pigeon pie. I've had a fulfilling and interesting career. But possibly the most rewarding aspect of my job is that I get to model clothes.

I love to experience the shapes, the textures, and the fabrics of the latest trends. But one thing my twenty years did not prepare me for is designers in the fashion industry who repeatedly stretch the boundaries with immodest clothing. I've seen shorts and skirts get shorter and tighter, and tops get smaller. I've seen jeans purposefully designed to reveal a woman's undergarments, see-through blouses that expose her bra, and slogans on T-shirts that exploit the girls who wear them. It makes me wonder, where does it end? The sad part is that girls who follow fashion (like me) sometimes adopt these trends without realizing the impact it has on their self-esteem, their families, the opposite sex, and their testimonies.

This led me to ask myself a serious question: Can I—a clothes-horse—and other fashion-forward girls have the freedom to dress trendy and fashionably in accordance with today's styles and still maintain the virtue of modesty?

The answer to that question is a resounding, "Yes!" But I had to learn *how*. And that's the purpose of this book: to pass on my findings to you, my fashion disciple. But as we get started, there is another lingering question we must answer: what *is* modesty? One of the first things I did when I started this journey was discover what modesty means in some other cultures and to the generations that came right before us.

I'd like to describe the first area I looked at as *cultural modesty*. In many Middle Eastern countries, modest attire is a hooded wrap called a *burqa* that covers a woman from head to toe, revealing only her eyes. It is worn over her daily clothes and is removed when she returns to her home. In some parts of Afghanistan and northwest Pakistan, the women even cover their eyes with a mesh grille. Due to political instability in these areas, women must adhere to this dress as a matter of personal safety. That's not fashion freedom!

In Indian cultures, one of the most expressive pieces in a woman's wardrobe is the feminine and modest *sari*. It's changed some through the generations but remains a modest statement in Indian cultures. One of the earliest depictions of the sari dates back to about 100 BC. This style of body wrapping may have evolved from the ancient temple dancers who danced in similar garments that allowed them to move without restraint, yet still remain modest.

Years ago I was shooting for an English magazine in Marrakesh, Morocco. Hands down, this was one of my favorite jobs. Everywhere I turned there were vibrant colors, the scent of curry and other spices, snake charmers, and locals traveling by camel. We were there from the end of July to the beginning of August, and it averaged 112 degrees Fahrenheit during the day. Most days I shot in the outskirts of the Sahara Desert or on the backs of beautiful white Arabian horses. Because of the intense heat, we took long breaks in the afternoon to go into Morocco's largest, traditional open-air market, or *souk*. I can't think of a better time to wear a tank top and shorts, but the women of our group were advised by our guide to follow certain wardrobe traditions. I had to hide my long blonde hair in a scarf, wear long linen pants, and completely cover my arms. It was so hot! But our guide insisted only prostitutes dress "immodestly." Rebelling against this cultural modesty could have literally endangered my life.

Second, there is *historical modesty*. Victorian attire came about during the reign of Queen Victoria of England. The dress varied quite a bit but with one common theme: the long, ankle-length skirt. After that, a woman's wardrobe always consisted of petticoats and bonnets, and until the beginning of the twentieth century, it was considered risqué to let your ankles show! Not much freedom there either!

In more recent generations, skirts became shorter, but conservative women would still wear knee-length to ankle-length skirts. Poodle skirts were knee- to mid-calf length and rounded out the decade of the 1950s. Modest trends like these lasted until the late 1960s when fashion was coupled with rebellion and the miniskirt was introduced. From there, the way women viewed fashion shifted; it became liberal. Suddenly there were bikinis, tight-fitting clothes, short shorts (appropriately called "hot pants"), and lots and *lots* of cleavage. It is no coincidence this rebellion also brought with it rampant drug use, promiscuous sex, and new sexually transmitted diseases. This is where our society's fashion made a spiraling downhill turn, and we're still suffering the consequences of it today.

Today's fashion has only gotten more revealing, which leads me to believe it's not so much our clothes (or lack thereof), but where our hearts are. What's going through the mind of a woman as she shops the latest trends? The answer, of course, depends on the *heart* of the woman. That is the starting point of this study . . . the heart. We'll be taking the road less traveled to get to our heart issues, make camp there, and listen for God's still, small voice. There we'll find many truths. We'll find modesty is a virtue that ignites a woman's dignity and respect for herself. It takes more courage to dress modestly and know one's value and worth stems from her Creator than to follow the patterns of the world and its skin-baring trends.

I want to show we can have the freedom to dress without rules, maintain our love for shopping, not get discouraged while shopping, and satisfy our craving for style without sacrificing our integrity. When our hearts are akin to Christ's, we'll develop a pattern that surpasses every fashion!

But I, for one, know it's not always easy to go against the grain and set yourself apart from the crowd. Trust me, I've had to walk off sets that wanted me to promote less-than-modest wardrobes. As you read, I'll be sharing how those decisions cost me huge campaigns, regular clients, and future work. It didn't make me popular, and it frustrated my clients and my agent, but God has been faithful to protect my career and my reputation.

Fashion should be fun, spontaneous, and should enable women to express themselves. But a good model (or role model) does not have to sacrifice her purity, dignity, or worth on the altar of bad taste!

He says . . .

> Therefore, I urge you, brothers, in view of God's mercy, to offer your bodies as living sacrifices, holy and pleasing to God—this is your spiritual act of worship. Do not conform any longer to the pattern of this world, but be transformed by the renewing of your mind. Then you will be able to test and approve what God's will is—his good, pleasing and perfect will.
>
> —ROMANS 12:1–2

So there it is: God's instruction for us to give our bodies to Him and for it to be "a living sacrifice holy and pleasing to God." As we will learn in this study, God desperately cares about *how* we present ourselves. God's Word goes on to say we are not to "conform any longer to the pattern of this world." Or as the New Living Translation phrases it, we should not "copy the behavior and customs of this world." How's that for specific? We aren't supposed to be like, act like, or even dress like the world around us. Does that mean we're supposed to wear long, flowing robes or paper sacks? Of course not! But it doesn't take long to see what the world dresses like. We all know we live in a skin-is-in society, and we have heard the phrase "Sex sells." Those are the kinds of behaviors and customs the Bible is talking about.

This does not, however, mean we can't dress fashionably or follow the trends (thank goodness!). In fact, in Proverbs 31, we learn of a lady who wears fine linen and is dressed in purple. That was one of the most expensive and trendy garments of her day! She was definitely fashion forward! But I have no doubt she knew modesty was more significant than her beautiful threads. These are some of the issues we'll be discussing in this book. But for now, as I mentioned before, our part starts with a heart willing to obey.

Maybe you picked up this book to read on your own or are reading this with a study group. Hopefully you're truly interested in what the Bible says about modesty. Either way, God knew you were going to be here, and He has a message for you. God wants His best for our lives, and that includes how we represent Him *and* ourselves by the way we dress.

The purpose of obedience is not simply for us to follow certain rules . . . that's called religion. The real purpose is to bring us into a better relationship with God . . . that's freedom! Obeying God's Word doesn't bind us; it sets us free!

One important thing to remember is that the Bible was not written in English as we read it today. Using a concordance, which is an index that lists significant words, their meanings, and scriptural references, we can go back to the original text and learn what the Author intended to convey so the true meaning isn't lost in translation. Throughout this book, I will refer to the Greek or Hebrew meaning of words so that we can see what the Bible says in its original form. These words are the building blocks on which we'll make our fashion decisions.

The first word is *legalism*. Legalism is the emphasis on outward actions (not inner changes) and the belief that those actions produce *rightness* with God. What it produces instead is a feeling of self-righteousness where we glorify our own actions instead of glorifying God. It also produces a condemnation of others, believing our good deeds (instead of pure hearts) bring us into a closer relationship with God. It's important for us to understand this is a dangerous trap because it keeps us works-oriented. And like any trap, it binds us and keeps us from total freedom.

The second term is *license*. License is the belief that we as Christians can do anything we please without consequence because we're already forgiven. This is another dangerous snare because our actions influence others, either positively or negatively, and can lead others *to* Christ or *away* from Christ. Having a false sense of license can come with some heavy and burdensome consequences.

The third word is *holiness*. Holiness can seem like a scary word because it's the chief attribute that describes God. However, did you know He calls *us* to be holy (1 Peter 1:15–16)? The word in Greek is *hagios* (pronounced hag-ee-os). It comes from a similar word, *hagnos* (pronounced hag-nos), which means "clean," "innocent," "modest," and "pure."[1] Thankfully you don't have to take my word for it. You can take God's Word for it. God desires for us to be holy and modest.

Of course we can't be holy on our own merit, but we can rely on Him to change our hearts. Now reread Romans 12:1–2. Understanding Scripture will help us know God the way *He* wants us to know Him. Will you join me in agreeing with God to have an open heart that listens and is willing to obey? I hope you will! I did, and it has changed the way I think, just as Romans 12:2 promises. And according to the end of the passage it's only then that we learn God's will for us. If I've learned one thing in life, it's that I want to know God's will for me!

So . . . what do you say?

Let me just tell you how honored I am to have you join me on this adventure! If you're like me, you love God and you love clothes; how wonderful it is that we can join the two and together discover God's best for our lives! Please feel free to be honest about your thoughts on this subject. You will get a chance to journal those thoughts in this section and discuss with your group your ideas, fears, struggles, victories, and hesitations. Just be yourself, and trust that God is walking through this with us!

Love, Rachel

1. How does it make you feel when you see a man stare at an immodestly dressed woman? Insecure? Jealous? Angry? Something else? Explain:

....

....

....

2. When that happens do you wish it were you getting the attention?

....

....

....

3. We see guys gawking at immodesty all the time. What do you think is going on in their hearts? What do you think is going on in the females' hearts?

....

....

....

4. We've already started talking about modesty as an issue that begins in the heart. Read Proverbs 21:2 and Proverbs 27:19. Discuss with your group; then write what these verses mean to you.

....

....

....

5. Read 1 Corinthians 10:23. Freedom can be positive or negative. At the beginning of this chapter, Seth noted his sisters have the confidence and freedom to dress modestly. The Bible is clear. Just because something is permissible does not mean it is beneficial or constructive. Freedom outside the boundaries of Scripture is license.

In your own words, what does *license* mean?

....

....

6. What are some things we can do as Christians that are *permissible* but not *beneficial*?

....

....

7. License isn't love for God, but a method of using God. This is a dangerous place to be in your spiritual walk. Why do you suppose that's true?

....

....

8. However, the same is true with legalism. *Legalism* is just a fancy word for trying so hard to please God that we start making up additional rules not found in Scripture. Can you imagine? Adding to God's Word? Why would this be a dangerous place to be?

....

....

....

This is why God wants us to live our lives according to His will without exploiting His Word or changing it to fit our lifestyle. Additionally, He doesn't want us to make a list of unscriptural standards we think God wants us to keep. There is no freedom in either of these choices.

Instead, we can find balance by honestly seeking what the Bible says about our choices and allowing God to change us from the inside out. That's where we'll find true freedom!

My Commitment:

Today, I promise to make the commitment to have an open heart about what God teaches through His Word on the issue of modesty. I will ask God to open my eyes and ears to see and hear His truths and to give me the courage it takes to obey.

Signed: _____ Date: _____

Verse Memorization: Romans 12:1–2

Therefore, I urge you, brothers, in view of God's mercy, to offer your bodies as living sacrifices, holy and pleasing to God—this is your spiritual act of worship. Do not conform any longer to the pattern of this world, but be transformed by the renewing of your mind. Then you will be able to test and approve what God's will is—his good, pleasing and perfect will.

Signed: _____ Date: _____

Lord Jesus, I thank You for these young women whom You adore. Thank You for Your work in their lives and for the work You will continue to do as we seek Your will and purpose for each of us on this important issue. We know You alone see our hearts, and

You alone judge whether or not they are pure. Create in us pure hearts, O God, and help our hearts and minds to be open to Your leading as we seek to obey. We love You, Lord. In Jesus' name, amen.

—Rachel

Fashioned by Forgiveness

Photo by Shane Greene

Tyler
Age: 16
State: North Carolina
Interests: lacrosse, baseball, golf, fishing
Future ambition: professional athlete

he says . . .

When I was younger I never noticed what girls were wearing. Kids don't usually take notice of things like that. But now that I'm sixteen, it seems I notice every little thing. It's so hard for us guys to look away and keep our hearts and eyes pure. My parents taught me modesty is important because the way a girl dresses draws the eyes of others, whether she knows it or not.

As an athlete of various sports, I've seen, in person and in the media, how ladies act and dress to get attention from the stars. Most of the girls in this situation are treated according to the way they portray themselves. If she is dressing immodestly—even if she does get attention—typically she is not respected. If she dresses modestly, usually two things happen: the wrong guys lose interest, and she receives respect from guys who know how to treat her. That's why it's so important for Christian girls to represent God's standard.

God doesn't want you to dress immodestly like other girls do; He wants you to set a positive standard for them to follow. The way you act and the style of clothes you wear interest guys who are attracted to that behavior and style, whatever they may be. One example I thought of was fishing. Certain lures are used to attract certain types of fish. In the same way, how you decide to dress and act will attract certain types of guys. Guys are visual creatures. So the style and fit of all your clothes—even bathing suits—combined with your actions are very powerful lures. So take note of how you dress and how you act. Remember you are *always* fishing.

—Tyler

she says . . .

First Samuel 16:7 says, "Man looks at the outward appearance, but the LORD looks at the heart!"

This passage used to bring me comfort whenever I felt like others were judging me. I would smile inwardly and quote the verse to myself. (Can you hear the "ha ha!" tone in my voice?) It wasn't until much later that God revealed my true motives and everything that was in my heart. My pride, selfishness, and sense of entitlement became more obvious to me the closer I walked with the Lord. This included my wardrobe. I struggled with it—I really did. And in this study you may too. We're so often taught not to worry about what others think about us. And I didn't. If I liked it, I wore it . . . get over it. Then, as I thought of this verse, something strange happened. I was terrified God *did* see my heart. The verse no longer brought me comfort, but shame. I knew what lurked deep down, and it wasn't pretty. Even though others might not have known, God knew.

This is when God pierced my heart about modesty. About ten years into my career, I was asked to model a bra for a department store catalog. I had never modeled lingerie before but wasn't dead set against it. I justified it, telling myself, "Even Christian women wear lingerie." Besides, this wasn't smutty underwear—it was full-coverage lingerie. I booked the job without counting the cost, and the pictures came out in Sunday's paper.

During this time, I was just about to launch the ministry *Modeling Christ*. I went to my pastor, Dr. Ruffin Snow, to seek an endorsement, but instead he gently prompted me to consider just *what* I had been modeling. He confronted me, in love but with firmness, on appearing in the lingerie advertisements. I felt stubborn and immovable, but I told him I would pray about it. I must confess I didn't understand because I felt the clothes were *modest*. What irony. This is how I know *modest* is a relative term. It means different things to different people.

My pastor proceeded to tell me men think differently than

women do, and that even though the garments weren't revealing to me, they still had the potential to make men stumble. I wondered just how that was *my* problem. He went on to tell me many men had come to him in need of counseling because they were struggling with pornography. At this point I began to feel anger because my modeling was definitely *not* pornography. As he gently continued, he shared with me most of these Christian men admitted their lusting and stumbling began with the images seen in a typical Sunday paper . . . the kind of images I was appearing in. The way I heard it—and the way he intended it—was that these kinds of ads were an introduction to pornography. One thing I understood for certain: men *do* think differently than women.

I prayed about it, but I struggled with the concept. I wrestled with the idea of needing to change the way I dressed because of the potential my choices had in making someone else falter in his faith or in aiding pornography. But the more I prayed and sincerely *wanted* to know God's will, the more my heart became convicted of the matter. My heart was changed, not because of my pastor (though God used him to initiate it), but because God cares about this issue. God *did* create men to be different from women. Perhaps one reason is so when we're wives, our husbands will keep adoring our bodies. That adoration can positively influence our self-esteem. However, if we as wives flaunt our bodies in public, then we set up our husbands for jealousy, and that can lead to all kinds of problems in a marriage. A marriage should be safe from those issues, and a husband should feel his wife's body belongs to his eyes and no others'.

When I accepted this standard and asked for God's forgiveness (for my unyielding spirit and for any damage I may have already caused another), I realized I'd have to explain to my agency I would no longer be available to model lingerie. This was a difficult task because I feared their judgment. Fortunately, they appreciated my honesty and conviction and removed it from my status list.

However, not long after that, I was on a booking for a national catalog that paid $1,500 a day. The client's demographic (the women they advertise to) was forty-five- to sixty-five-year-old women. The wardrobe consisted mostly of sweaters and trousers, but they had to do a makeup shot they missed the day before. It was a bra. A large granny-panty bra, but a bra none the less. Since I was the only model booked, they asked me to shoot it. I squirmed and shifted but knew my answer had to be no. I expected them to appreciate my moral compass as my agency did, but this was not the case. They were angry. They called my booker and demanded I do the shot, or they'd let me go for the day and not have me back. This was extremely hard for me, but I stood my ground. I spoke with my agent, and God gave me the words:

"If my morals were for sale then I'd be a prostitute." I gasped at my audacity but found acceptance and respect from my booker. She spoke with the client and stood by my decision. I was dismissed and lost the client, but I gained something else that day . . . *dignity*.

Read Psalm 139:23–24.

Write the verses:

....

....

God cares about our hearts. He cares about our motives. Psalm 51:10 reflects a wonderful prayer we can use as we study this timely issue of modesty: *Create in me a pure heart, O God.* There is not a more simple prayer we can pray to surrender anew to Him daily.

He says . . .

> One evening David got up from his bed and walked around on the roof of the palace. From the roof he saw a woman bathing. The woman was very beautiful.
>
> —2 Samuel 11:2

When I read this passage, I feel like a fly on the wall of King David's palace. Try to get the picture in your head: Here's the young, mighty, influential, handsome king of Israel (1 Samuel 16:12). It's springtime; his entire army is at battle (2 Samuel 11:1). He's up in the late afternoon, walking around on the flat rooftop of his palace. From his perch his eyes glance over at a neighboring home where he sees the beautiful Bathsheba bathing. . . .

Okay, stop there. Let's get some perspective on this story. The beginning of this chapter in Samuel says it was a time when "kings go off to war" (v. 1). David was the king of Israel. Why wasn't he at his post leading his troops? Why was he instead walking around on his rooftop?

In many Middle Eastern countries people would get up early in the morning to work, but then take an afternoon nap at midday when the sun was at its hottest. (I experienced this while I was shooting for an English catalog in Spain. The entire city of

Barcelona shut down during what they called *siesta* because of the intense heat. We worked through it, however, and I modeled hooded fleece sweatshirts and sweatpants in the sweltering heat!) So, as I imagine it, David arose after his mid-afternoon nap to the much cooler evening and went to walk on his rooftop, probably something like a terrace. Keep in mind, it couldn't have been late evening or he wouldn't have been able to see her. There were many houses in Jerusalem, and some of them had a private, walled garden. Bathsheba may have had a bath in her garden, or she could have been bathing by an open window.

Not only was David in the wrong place at the wrong time (because he should have been with his men on the battlefield), but also many commentaries suggest Bathsheba wasn't totally innocent. Theologian David Guzik states, "There is little doubt that this woman (later called by the name *Bathsheba*) acted immodestly . . . *certainly* she knew that her bath was visible from the roof of the palace. Any immodesty on Bathsheba's part did not excuse David's sin, but she was still responsible for her wrong."[1] Bible commentator Adam Clarke states, "How could any woman of delicacy expose herself where she could be so fully and openly viewed? Did she not know that she was at least in view of the king's terrace?"[2]

This reminds me of those stickers I see on the backs of transfer trucks: IF YOU CAN'T SEE MY MIRRORS, I CAN'T SEE YOU. Obviously, then, the opposite is true: if you *can* see the mirrors, the driver *can* see you. So if David had enough of a view of Bathsheba to see she was beautiful, she no doubt could see the roof of his palace, where he would have frequently been on cool evenings.

Once I read a pastor's commentary that supposed she must

have been foolish, rebellious, or needy for attention. Now isn't that a perfect picture of immodesty in today's society? Even Christian young women can fall into one of these three categories when we dress immodestly. Foolish, rebellious, or needy for attention. Where would you fall? At one time or another, I have been each of these. As a young Christian I would've belonged to the category of *foolish*, wearing what was in style without any realization it could be hindering a fellow believer. When people finally brought it to my attention, I made excuses and, being *rebellious*, I believed it was their problem. If they didn't like what I was wearing, they shouldn't look. During lapses of self-esteem I would've been *needy for attention*. I got plenty of attention in those days for my attire, but not the kind that would glorify God. The sad part is that I've been at all three stages and all while I was a Christian. That's embarrassing! So no matter where you are or have been, I've been there too. Let's just not stay there!

James 1:15 teaches, "After desire has conceived, it gives birth to sin; and sin, when it is full-grown, gives birth to death." David indeed had desire for Bathsheba, and it did, as Scripture promises, give birth to sin. His gazing turned to staring, then lusting. David's sin was not in *seeing* Bathsheba; it was in choosing to *keep* seeing her.

My husband and best friend, Daryl, is a great example for young men of how not to do this. He is a former college athlete, and we love to watch sports on the big screen at home. However, with televised sports often come immodest, scantily clad women on the sidelines or on commercials. He chooses to purposefully turn his head away from the screen when he sees them. Does he do this because he's afraid he will cheat on me? No. He does it because he knows what James 1:15 teaches, and he loves his Savior and his wife.

But there's more to the verse—and more to the story. After David lusted after Bathsheba, he sent messengers to get her (not forcefully, but probably persuasively), and he slept with her (2 Samuel 11:4). Uh-oh. That was not good. First of all, David was married (1 Samuel 25:42–43; 2 Samuel 3:2–5). Bathsheba was married as well, and David knew it. After watching her bathe, he had inquired about her and discovered she was married to one of his most prominent soldiers, Uriah (2 Samuel 11:3). But that didn't stop him. He still pursued her, and she got pregnant. And then to make matters worse, in order to cover his sin(s), David ordered one of his finest and most God-honoring soldiers (Uriah) to be put on the front lines of war where he was killed in battle.

Remember James 1:15: "and sin, when it is full-grown, gives birth to death"? It all came to fruition just as God's Word said it would. We may not have any idea how far-reaching an impact our choices will have, but God's Word warns us there are consequences to them. It makes me think of all the times I dressed in a way that served myself or attempted to draw attention to my body. Did my freedom cause devastation to another? I often ask in my small groups, "If you're dressed modestly and a guy lusts after you, who does God hold accountable?" The answer, of course, is always, "The guy." Then I ask, "If you are dressed *immodestly* and a guy lusts after you, who does God hold accountable?" The answer is *both*.

I want to close on a lighter note, with another true story: Years ago, I was interested in a guy at Bible college, and we wrote sweet letters back and forth during our times away on ministry. One day, as we often did, I signed my name with a Bible verse reference. This time it was 1 Samuel 12:24, which says, "But be sure to fear the LORD and serve him faithfully with all your heart; consider what great things he has done for you." I was proud of the "new" verse I'd found and was sure my gentleman friend would be impressed too.

After I passed the note along to the messenger who would later deliver it, I decided to go back and underline the reference in my Bible. I turned to 2 Samuel 12:24 and was devastated when I read what it said: "Then David comforted his wife Bathsheba, and he went to her and lay with her."

Oh my goodness! Had I just signed my name along with a reference to extra-marital sex? Can you see my eyes popping out of their sockets and the sweat pouring from my head? I raced to the messenger to intercept the letter. Praise God, I had actually put the correct reference, but I gave my roommates a story to laugh at for weeks!

> David looked at Bathsheba and said "beauty" but God saw this as *ugly*. The pleasures of sin deceive us like the bait hides the hook. We must call it what God calls it—sin. We want to say "affair" but God says "adultery." We want to say, "love" but God says "lust." We want to say "sexy" but God says "sin." We want to say, "romantic" but God says "ruin." We want to say, "destiny" but God says "destruction."
>
> —David Guzik[3]

So . . . what do you say?

We're just getting started, but can you believe how much the Bible has to say on the subject of modesty, lust, and the heart? It's amazing how much we can find in the Scriptures if we put our minds to the task of uncovering the riches within. I love Luke 11:9. Here it is in the King James Version: "Ask, and it shall be given you; seek, and ye shall find; knock, and it shall be opened unto you." Do you know He has much more in store for us as we study His Word together? I'm encouraged you're with me, and I know He will deliver on His promise in Luke 11:9!

1. Why do you think God made men to be tempted by visuals more than women are? Explain:

....

....

2. In Dannah Gresh's book *Secret Keeper*, she explains, "It's not '*just*' fashion, but a constant source of spiritual failure for men."[4] How does it make you feel to have the power to seduce a man simply by what you wear? Responsible? Nervous? Empowered? Afraid? Annoyed? Something else?

....

....

3. Discuss the word *sexy* with the group. What does it mean? When do you think it's appropriate?

....

....

4. Read Daniel 11:35. Who does the passage say may stumble?

....

....

I don't know about you, but I am grateful to read even the "wise will stumble." None of us are perfect because, if we were, we wouldn't need a Savior. I must admit, sometimes I wouldn't consider my actions a stumble but rather a big ol' trip-and-careen-to-the-ground-smearing-my-face-on-the-sidewalk fall. For instance, in those foolish, rebellious, needy-for-attention immodest moments. Will you join me in repentance for those times and commit to obeying the Word of the Lord where this subject is concerned? We're in this together, girlfriend!

> I cannot and will not cut my conscience to fit this year's fashions.
> —Lillian Hellman, May 19, 1952[5]

We've been studying how, centuries ago, authors under the inspiration of God wrote of the effects of modesty and immodesty. In the quote above we read of a lady who refused to set aside her own principles to please others. How easy or difficult is it, or will it be, for you to choose modesty as a way of life?

....

....

. . . .

. . . .

Verse Memorization: Luke 11:9, KJV

Ask, and it shall be given you; seek, and ye shall find; knock, and it shall be opened unto you.

Signed: _____ Date: _____

Lord, please help me overcome the immodest fashion temptations this world offers us. And when I am acting foolish, rebellious, or needy for attention, God help me to turn to You for wisdom and truth. In Jesus' name, amen.

—Rachel

Chapter Three

Fashioned for Favor

Photo by Jordan Parker

Tommy

Age: 19
State: New York
Interests: snowboarding, wake surfing
Future ambition: action sports ministry

he says . . .

When I see a girl dressed modestly but with style, one word comes to mind: *respect*. In today's society so much is focused around respect—everyone wants it, yet not everyone is willing to give it.

Every guy is looking for a cute, respectable girl. One of the first ways to determine if a girl is respectable is to determine whether or not she respects herself. I'm sure I have no idea how difficult it is for girls to find modest clothing in the immodest world we live in, but I know when girls *do* dress modestly, it shows they value their character and have respect for themselves.

While I don't fully understand the challenges a girl faces not only finding, but also deciding to wear modest clothing, I don't think girls can truly understand the way a guy's mind works as it relates to this issue either. I can tell you from experience that the way a girl dresses can definitely help or hinder a guy's spiritual walk. As hard as we try to train our minds and our eyes to avoid lust, the smallest little immodesty can still become a severe stumbling block—even for the strongest of guys. I refuse to justify my sins by blaming it on the way a girl chooses to dress, but please realize guys are fighting a spiritual battle (one you will want your future husband to be victorious in fighting as well). So if you dress immodestly, you are truly "dressed to kill."

Ladies, we're not asking you to walk around in rain ponchos! Just know when guys look at an immodestly dressed girl, they are not only thinking of how cute she looks. They are sinning in their minds. And if you have any doubt about whether or not a guy will notice you in modest attire, let me assure you, he will. Guys who recognize the effort it takes to dress modestly in a culture dominated by sexuality will respect you even more for your efforts. Plus, I know many guys like me who find modesty far more attractive.

—Tommy

she says . . .

One of the most wonderful things about being in the modeling industry for so long is that I've been able to travel the world. Thirty countries and forty-one states to be exact. Some experiences have been great, while others have been quite challenging. One situation in particular comes to mind: I was working in Athens, Greece. It was February, cold, and rainy, not at all what I expected from the post-card picturesque images I'd seen before I arrived. But I was there to work, not vacation. My agenda was to get as many "tear sheets" as possible for my portfolio. Tear sheets are published pictures of the model she tears out of magazines for her portfolio. More tear sheets mean more experience, and in return more clients want to book her for jobs. The more jobs she gets, the more in demand she is, and subsequently she receives a higher income.

The day after I arrived I went into my agency to introduce myself in person. Until then they'd only seen pictures of me. It took some time to find them, partly because everything was written in Greek and partly because I had no idea what to look for. Finally, I found them on a tiny street (that wasn't even on the map) right below the ruins of the Acropolis. This is my favorite area in Athens. It's so rich in history, archaeology, and memories of the apostle Paul's teaching at Mars Hill. In the shadow of the Acropolis lies an area called "Plaka." It's like a village within the city, and it's a maze of winding streets featuring every kind of souvenir one could hope for. Since my agency was right there, I knew I'd be seeing a lot of this shoppers' paradise.

I made my way up the three-hundred-year-old stairs to meet my new bookers. They spoke broken and complicated English, but

I could understand them. After all, their English was far better than my Greek. They hugged me and welcomed me to their country and were anxious to get me out to see their clients. I handed them my most up-to-date portfolio, and they quickly went to the task of choosing the pictures they would put on my composite card. A composite card is a quick reference card, similar to a business card, that a model hands out to clients to be remembered. It usually consists of a headshot on the front, four pictures on the back, along with their agency affiliation, height, and measurements. Once the pictures were selected, I would be off to the printers to have hundreds of copies made. While I waited for them to compare images, I decided it would be a good time to explain to my new employer there were certain types of jobs I wouldn't do. It's always a bit intimidating for someone to purposely put oneself into the position of being different—and I am no exception. It's hard. But I knew my testimony could be at stake, and it was important for us to be on the same page.

I explained I wouldn't be casting for any lingerie jobs, anything nude or sheer, no alcohol or cigarette ads, and nothing perverse, provocative, or subliminal. If I close my eyes, I can still remember my agent's face as she tried to wrap her mind around my words. Cigarette in hand, she raised her eyebrows and said, "You won't work." After a brief, awkward silence I simply smiled and said, "Okay, then I'll go shopping." She touched my arm to keep me from leaving as she spoke in her thick Grecian accent: "We try."

Whew! I had done it. We were on the same page. She rattled off something in her native tongue to the other bookers who were looking at me like I was crazy, but they hesitantly agreed to work with my requests. We smiled and I left.

That night I received a fax at the hotel where I was staying for the next six weeks. It was my agenda for the following day, a list of castings and go-sees (a term coined in the modeling industry referring to a client I would *go and see*). There were familiar names listed: *Elle, Marie Claire*, and L'Oreal. Also on the list was a popular magazine in Europe, *Lipstick*. Here is an excerpt from an e-mail I wrote to my mom after my castings:

> At *Lipstick*, they really liked me and asked me to try on an outfit. So I followed her into the room, while the other models waited. She pulled out a sheer thong and sheer bra. I said, "I'm sorry, but I won't model that." She said, "Okay, bye." When I walked out, the others girls were like, "What happened?" I said, "I don't need tear sheets that bad." My only regret is that I prefaced it by saying "I'm sorry. . . ." Ugh! I'm not sorry! Are they crazy? If this is what it's all cracked up to be, then they can keep their tear sheets. Ok, I'm done. Just had to vent. The younger girls don't get it. It's so sad. Don't they realize they have a choice? They say, "Oh, but it's beautiful." Yeah, maybe to you—but not to the sleazebag who'll be looking at you. So if I don't leave Greece with tear sheets, I'll leave with my integrity.
>
> Love and miss you, Rachel

Well, let's fast-forward a bit. Fortunately, I *did* leave Greece with tear sheets, *and* my integrity. God also blessed the time I was there with many opportunities to share the gospel with Russian and Polish refugees, other models, and my roommates. He blessed my work, and, although I drew my line in the sand about what I wouldn't model, I worked more than anyone expected and more than my fellow models. God did that. Not my agency, not me . . . God. I had a new slogan: God is my agent.

> It is easier to keep temptation at a distance, than to resist it when near.
>
> —Bible Commentator Matthew Henry[1]

He says . . .

> But Daniel resolved not to defile himself with the royal food and wine, and he asked the chief official for permission not to defile himself this way.
>
> —DANIEL 1:8

Daniel is one of my favorite books of Scripture. It has much to say about prophecy and the return of our Lord Jesus, but it also has rich stories about the life of a cute teenage boy from Jerusalem named Daniel.

The book of Daniel opens as his homeland is besieged by the king of Babylon. After plundering Jerusalem, King Nebuchadnezzar (I call him "Nebby") orders the chief of his officials to bring young Hebrew men from the royal family or nobility to serve in his palace. Not just any teenage boys, those chosen had to be handsome, intelligent, educated, and wise. (It would be like you or me being forced to move to an enemy nation to be their ruler's right-hand assistant.) However, royalty had an image to preserve. Daniel and his buddies couldn't be seen alongside the king as the scrawny, skinny young men they were. It was important for them to look the part, so the king ordered these boys to be fattened up with delicacies from his table (Daniel 1:5).

Because Daniel was a faithful Jew who honored God, there were some things that would not have been appropriate for him to participate or partake in. This was an issue because King Nebby was pagan and worshiped a false god. The meat wouldn't have been slain according to the Mosaic Law Daniel followed and would have been offered as a sacrifice to the king's idol. Consuming it would have been dangerously forbidden by Daniel's faith.

King Nebby assigned the four young men to eat from the king's table for three years. But even though Daniel was in another country—and in another culture—he knew *whom* he belonged to and represented. He loved God too much to straddle the fence, even when his job was in jeopardy. He purposed in his heart that he would not defile his body (Daniel 1:8).

This story reminds me of Greece. Just like Daniel, I was in another country and another culture, but I knew *whom* I belonged to and represented. I, like Daniel, could have easily justified, "It's just the nature of the business," or "Who would know?" And just like Daniel's, my job was in jeopardy. But God protected me and urged me to purpose in my heart not to defile myself.

So back to Daniel. He went to the chief official for permission not to defile himself. The official told Daniel he was afraid to comply with his request for fear the king would notice Daniel looking worse than the other young men. If this happened King

Nebby would have the official's head! So Daniel offered the guard this test: "Please test your servants for ten days: Give us nothing but vegetables to eat and water to drink. Then compare our appearance with that of the young men who eat the royal food, and treat your servants in accordance with what you see" (Daniel 1:12–13). The guard agreed and tested them for ten days.

At the end of ten days the young men looked healthier and more nourished than any of the other young men who ate from the king's table (Daniel 1:15). On top of all that, God blessed them intellectually as well! God granted them favor, and at the end of the set time, the chief official presented them to King Nebby (Daniel 1:17–18). After talking with them, the king found none equaled Daniel and the other three young Hebrew men, and he observed they were ten times better than those already serving in his court!

Just like the story of Daniel, even though my standards were unreasonable to my agent, God blessed me with favor. No matter the century, the Bible teaches in Hebrews 11:6 that God rewards those who earnestly seek Him. He loves to show off in this way, so we and everyone else knows *He* did it. Not King Nebby's chief official, not my agent in Greece, but *Him*.

After this, the king placed Daniel in a high position and lavished many gifts on him. He even made him ruler over the entire province of Babylon (Daniel 2:48). King Nebby was still pagan—as presumably were my Greek agents—but God still granted favor so those watching could see there was something different about Daniel and his friends.

Hezekiah, the twelfth king of Judah, must have also known something about obedience to God and the blessings it brings. In

2 Chronicles 31:21, we read this: "In everything that he undertook in the service of God's temple and in obedience to the law and the commands, he sought his God and worked wholeheartedly. And so he prospered." Who do you think prospered him? The One to whom he was obedient.

Daniel's decision could very well have cost him his life. My decision could have slammed the brakes on my career. Your decision to commit yourself to an obedient life of modesty could cost you . . . hmm. What could it cost you? Friends? Fashion? Ego? And what could choosing not to obey cost you? God's blessings? Your self-respect?

One thing I have learned about dressing provocatively is women who seek attention with this method often receive it, but always at the expense of their self-esteem. It becomes a cycle of attention from men for their bodies, and though they feel a rush from that attention, it leaves them feeling empty, lacking, and hungry for another rush to "fix" their need again. Consequently, skirts continue to get shorter and tops get tighter. That's the way sin works in our lives as well. We hunger for it, but before long, it leaves us feeling empty and desperate for more.

In my own experience, once I surrendered and broke my pattern of immodesty, my obedience reversed the cycle. My eyes were finally open to what I stubbornly ignored for so long. Now I'm more sensitive to what I wear, I have a much healthier self-image, and I don't have to fear the consequential damage I could cause another.

Daniel's story is an inspiration and encouragement to all Christians who choose to live in obedience to the Word of God in spite of the potential consequences. It may be that *everyone else* wears short shorts and *everyone else* shows a little cleavage, but you, sweet friend, can purpose in your heart not to defile yourself. Dare to be a Daniel—or more appropriately, a *Danielle*.

So . . . what do you say?

It amazes me how God gives us examples to follow from Scriptures—like the story of Daniel—and blesses us, often in the same ways, when we follow His plan. And that's just *one* of the ways God is faithful. We can trust He has our best interest in mind. We fail when we let our guard down and allow the world into our hearts. Satan would have been thrilled if Daniel and his three friends had decided to "go with the flow" as the other Hebrew boys had done. And he would be just as pleased for us to do the same. The Bible teaches: "Be self-controlled and alert. Your enemy the devil prowls around like a roaring lion looking for someone to devour" (1 Peter 5:8). If we are saved, Satan cannot have us, only try to trip us up. We cannot be possessed, only oppressed. We belong to Christ, and no one, not even Satan, can take us away from Him (John 10:29). This is important for believers to know because we *will* trip up. We *will* sin. But we can come back into fellowship with God by seeking His forgiveness or, in theological terms, *repenting*. Let's not let our guards down. Instead, let's remember *whose* we are, and whose we will forever be!

1. If Satan can't have us once we're saved, why does he even attempt to mess with us?

....

....

....

2. Do you think Daniel was tempted to go along with the king's diet and not draw attention to himself? Have you ever been in this type of situation? What happened?

....

....

3. Notice in 1 Peter 5:8 we are warned to be "self-controlled and alert." Have you ever been in a situation when you let your guard down and did something you didn't intend to do?

....

....

Let me tell you about a time when I did:

In this chapter, I've shared with you a number of things I won't model because of my love for the Lord. Another is advertising alcohol. I am adamant about this. I've chosen not to drink socially either. Because of my convictions, I won't even model holding a glass of anything that *looks* like alcohol. However, a few years ago I was modeling in Egypt on a yacht, and the shot consisted of me standing on the deck with another model and a "butler" holding a tray of champagne. I informed the photography crew the butler could *present* the glass to me, but I would not touch it or even look at it. They snarled, but went ahead with the shot. As I was modeling I got in my zone as I always do, and they rattled off countless pictures. I placed my hand on my hip, then my neck, then glared out to sea, then shifted my weight, then cocked my head, then reached for the glass, then . . . WAIT! Did I just hold that glass? Man! I had slipped up, but it was just one of more than a hundred shots. Surely they wouldn't choose that one. Well, guess what? Do I even need to tell you? Yep, there's a published full-page color photo of me in an international magazine holding a glass of champagne. I never intended it to happen. (And no, I won't tell you which publication.) When it was published, I just shook my head. I couldn't believe I let my guard down for even a second. Satan got a kick out of it, for sure. But you know what? Satan still didn't win. He tried hard to silence my testimony and label me as a hypocrite. And he does it because he can't have me—all he can do is mess with me. But I'm not worried and neither should you be. God will take care of our enemy!

Verse Memorization: John 10:28–30

I give them eternal life, and they shall never perish; no one can snatch them out of my hand. My Father, who has given them to me, is greater than all; no one can snatch them out of my Father's hand. I and the Father are one.

Signed: _____ Date: _____

Thank You, Lord Jesus, that although Satan tries to humiliate and defeat us, he cannot snatch us from Your hand. Please help our eyes see the traps he sets before us that would make us stumble. Help us always be on guard and rush to You for redemption when we fail. You are so faithful! In Jesus' name, amen.

—Rachel

Chapter Four

Fashioned for Faithfulness

Photo by Richard Duncan

Cody
Age: 16
State: Florida
Interests: music, basketball
Future ambition: husband and father

Little girl fourteen flipping through a magazine
Says she wants to look that way
But her hair isn't straight her body isn't fake

And she's always felt overweight

Well little girl fourteen I wish that you could see
That beauty is within your heart
And you were made with such care your skin
Your body and your hair
Are perfect just the way they are
—Jonny Diaz, *More Beautiful You*[1]

he says . . .

Jonny Diaz's song emphasizes exactly what I would say to the young women reading this. God loves you (no matter what) for the *most* beautiful part of you . . . what's on the inside!

What the lyrics tell me is God cares more about how His daughter's *heart* looks than anything else. When young women dress immodestly, it sets up us Christian guys for our own demise and the Bible teaches the resulting desires will destroy us! Know this is something that affects not just me, but your future husband as well. As young men seeking God's best, we need to keep our sights on things of heaven and stay strong in the Lord, separated from this earth. It would be amazing if those who claim to be Christians would be modest in the way they dress and act, instead of focusing on being the most eye-popping thing in the room. Those who do this (whether intentionally or not) are saying, "Hey, I'm the next piece of meat for you, so come and get me!" Think about this as you go through your day: will you live for yourself, or live for what God wants you to be . . . the more beautiful you?

—Cody

she says . . .

(You may need to speak with your parents about the
following guidelines. Ultimately, the decision is theirs.
Please respect and adhere to their wishes.)

We've talked about what modesty means, how it's a heart issue, and some of the ramifications of living without it. We know first impressions are important and they're difficult to reverse, but how does one implement the specifics of modesty in her wardrobe? This chapter is going to focus on just that—specifics. Let's start with articles of clothing worn from the waist up.

First, we have to realize these are not rules, only *guidelines* for a modest fashion plate. These are specifics I utilize for myself and are my recommendations. Each of these is reliable and works with a *moving* body. Everyone knows we exist in many different positions. We stand, sit, reach, climb, raise our arms, jump, bend over, and crouch on the floor. Our clothing should move with our bodies and remain modest while in these various positions. Also, keep in mind sometimes, it's just easier to buy a size larger than we're used to. If the size label bothers you, just clip it out. So without further ado, here we go!

BRAS: Shirts should never be so tight we see the outline of undergarments beneath or so transparent we see the undergarments themselves. Bras are underwear, and underwear should never be considered *outerwear*. This means you even need to conceal your straps. It's important to have several bra types in your wardrobe for different style tops (a strapless, a racerback, and a traditional). Make sure you're fitted properly for your bras, so they're neither too tight and cause discomfort, nor too loose and unable to do their job. It's equally important to have flesh-colored bras that match your skin tone. Many women make the mistake of wearing a colored bra (or even a white bra) under light-colored clothes. A white bra under a white top almost always shows. Also, include bras in your wardrobe that are smooth (not textured) because this, too, can show through. Bras also need to be replaced as your body changes and with the typical wear and tear from washing machines.

Additionally, bras should be thick enough to conceal your body should you get wet unexpectedly or if the weather is cold. Sports bras are still bras and should never be worn alone. A simple fix is to add a modest tank top or T-shirt over the sports bra when you're working out. And remember the bigger your chest, the more support you'll need.

STRAPS ON SHIRTS: My rule of thumb is two finger-widths for straps. I still own some spaghetti-strap tops, but I only wear them under blazers, sweaters, or layered with other tank tops. You also have the option of complementing it with a shrug. Weddings and other formal occasions often make it more difficult to find modest straps, so use discretion, especially when covering your back and cleavage. And remember that a wedding is an event that should celebrate your purity.

MATERIAL AND FIT: Shirts should not be too thin, too tight, or too sheer. These fabrics draw unnecessary attention to your chest. Be especially careful with tops you wear to the gym. Many women seem to toss out these guidelines when they're working out. Don't forget when men work out their testosterone is flowing! This is an especially critical time to conceal, not reveal.

Tops that button in the front may gape open, giving those near you an irresistible invitation to peek inside. Shirts that are too large can also be immodest if the armholes are large enough to show your chest from a side view.

COVERAGE: Tops should not only express your individuality, but also cover you appropriately. Tube tops, cropped shirts, one-shoulder, and backless garments should not be considered modest. Bare backs can be a huge stumbling block for guys. (Let's spare these men God loves so much!) If your belly shows when you raise your arms, fix it by wearing a tank top or camisole underneath.

CLEAVAGE: Cleavage is just as alluring as the rest of your breasts and should be hidden *under* your clothing. I once met a woman at a convention who told me, "Modesty is easy . . . no cracks in the front or the back!" I couldn't have said it better! I have a simple trick that helps me every time I shop: place four fingers at the base of your collarbone. This is how low your neckline can be, without revealing your cleavage, even when you bend forward. I have thoroughly tested this and found any lower than this gives a tempting view of your chest when you lean over. Keep this in mind, especially if you're wearing a V-neck top that dips lower at the middle of your chest. Pair low-cut tops with a matching or coordinating top underneath.

WRITING: I'm perfectly fine with a sports logo or other writing on a shirt as long as the shirt isn't too tight. However, keep in mind when you wear a shirt with writing across the chest, people will stare at your bust to read the words. On the other hand, messages that are flirty or inappropriate are not an option, no matter where they're placed. Intentionally seeking this kind of attention is not only wrong, it's also self-exploiting.

ALLUSIONS: Even if you follow all the guidelines I've just mentioned, you could still create an immodest *allusion* with your clothing. Even with a layered shirt underneath, tops that are formfitting and button just under the bust draw immediate attention where it doesn't need to be. The same is true for sheer blouses even when paired with a camisole, especially if the camisole is lacy and mimics lingerie. Another example is a shirt with small pockets situated directly over each of your breasts. If you're well-endowed, a purse strap slung diagonally across your chest can also be immodest. Keep in mind, we might not catch everything, but the issue here is to be sensitive to the Holy Spirit when it comes to the allusions we present.

If you're feeling overwhelmed right about now, know I've been where you are. When God opened my eyes to what was hanging in my closet, I was overcome with apprehension, but I knew I had some business to attend to. Many things needed to either go or be given a new purpose. Slim-fitting outfits I once wore to the gym would only be worn to sleep in. Adorable spaghetti-strap tops would exist only under blazers or sweaters. Low-cut or cropped tops would forever have a companion . . . a layering undershirt. Each time I gained weight, I would have to reassess my wardrobe instead of trying my best to squeeze into something that didn't fit. Amazingly, the more I found new uses for otherwise inappropriate items, the more freedom I found in modesty.

Furthermore, I have a newfound appreciation for accessories! I found I didn't have to sacrifice my personal sense of style as I rearranged my wardrobe. The second part of Luke 12:33 states, "Provide purses for yourselves that will not wear out." Ok, I know that's *completely* out of context, but just for fun I drew a heart next to it in my Bible! Still, it reminds me we have lots of opportunities to express ourselves through accessories.

Bold bags and belts, cute clutches, slouchy scarves, textured tights, and high heels are just the tip of the proverbial iceberg!

Think of how many ways you can spruce up an outfit just with shoes . . . from knee-high boots to ballerina flats and every sort of material imaginable . . . canvas, plastic, leather, pleather!

Jewelry is another favorite of mine. I love earrings that make a bold statement. Sometimes I'll pair them with a necklace or bracelet. Jewelry can match your mood, the hardware on your outfit, or the color you're wearing. They can be shiny, dull, beaded, colorful, monotone, metal, basic, funky, or chunky. I have and utilize all of the above!

Sometimes, if I'm particularly bold, I'll wear a hat. I have a beret, a cowboy hat, a beanie, a fedora, felt hats, straw hats, visors, and caps. Some in every color!

The point is, there's a lot you can do to express yourself with accessories. My wardrobe is flattering and fashionable, and I accessorize to suit my latest whim. I've re-created many outfits in my closet, and now I don't ever have to wonder if someone is judging my intentions. I can shop with standards simply by ensuring my butt, boobs, and belly are covered. I can enjoy ever-changing styles without letting the season's trends dictate my convictions. More important, I've earned respect and now have the reputation of model *and* role model.

He says . . .

A good name is more desirable than great riches; to be esteemed is better than silver or gold.

—PROVERBS 22:1

What comes to mind when you see the words "a good name"? Do you think of *your* name? Of course, this verse isn't talking about our given names but what our names represent. The Hebrew word *name* here is *shem* (pronounced shame). It doesn't mean *shame*, though, in fact just the opposite. It means "honor," "character," and "fame," as in *reputation*. Now, reread the verse, replacing *name* with *reputation*.

Can you see how important a good name is in God's sight? He says it's more desirable than wealth! Yet, so many people don't cherish its value or work (and sometimes sacrifice) to protect it. There are many things that can reflect or influence your reputation. Your speech, your choices, the company you keep, even your clothing affect your reputation. Remember, when most people see a woman dressed provocatively they tend to assume certain things about her. And if they're distracted by her immodesty, they may never get a chance to assess her heart, personality, and character for what it's really worth. Thankfully there are at least five places in God's Word that show us how we *should* clothe ourselves.

In Psalm 45:3, we read, "Clothe yourself with splendor and majesty." This is a psalm written for a royal wedding. The Hebrew words for *splendor* and *majesty* here mean "beauty," "excellence," and "honor." So how we physically clothe ourselves should represent these attributes.

In Isaiah 52:1, the prophet is urging the people of Israel to *clothe* themselves with strength, which means to be strong and bold. When we are in a situation that could challenge our reputations, it's important for us to be strong under pressure because our decisions dictate not only what others think about us, but also our faith.

The apostle Paul says in Romans 13:14 to "clothe yourselves

with the Lord Jesus Christ, and do not think about how to gratify the desires of the sinful nature." Every time we satisfy our own sinful desires we negatively influence our reputations. But when we put on the nature of Christ by behaving in a way that pleases Him, we *positively* affect our reputations. That's why we must ask ourselves if our clothing choices would honor and represent Jesus.

Paul goes on to say, "Clothe yourselves with compassion, kindness, humility, gentleness and patience" (Colossians 3:12). It matters to God how we treat others. Do we show proper compassion for those who are less fortunate? Do we act in kindness to those who are not in our group of friends? Are we gentle in our words with our parents? Are we patient with our siblings? God teaches us a lot in Scripture about how we should clothe our bodies, but more often He addresses our heart and actions. The most modestly dressed girls can lack all of these things and therefore have reputations that displease the Lord.

Our final reference is 1 Peter 5:5: "Clothe yourselves with humility toward one another, because, 'God opposes the proud but gives grace to the humble.'" Notice this is the second reference in our list that addresses humility. Sometimes a girl can focus on the brands she wears and the cost of her clothes. Usually when she does this, it's so others will notice. This is not a position of humility. It's not wrong to want to wear brand names or expensive clothes; it's wrong to want everyone to notice.

God gives us specifics on how we should clothe ourselves to glorify Him. He teaches us how to have *and keep* a good name because of its influence on others. And we learn everything we wear can affect our reputations either positively or negatively. The question we should then ask is: "How does my dress label *me*?"

So . . . what do you say?

When I was in Bible college, we were challenged to ask God for a Scripture that could be our "life verse," a verse that would be our cornerstone and help define who God wanted us to become. I prayed about it, and God led me to 1 Peter 3:4, which teaches, "Instead, it should be that of your inner self, the unfading beauty of a gentle and quiet spirit, which is of great worth in God's sight." I had no idea some years later I would have a ministry and book devoted to this premise. But God obviously did!

I remember when, as a joke, I told the ladies in my dorm my life verse was Luke 15:23: "Bring the fattened calf and kill it. Let's have a feast and celebrate." I thought it was so funny and one of my roommates, Erin, jumped on board saying her verse would be Proverbs 30:20: "She eats and wipes her mouth and says, 'I've done nothing wrong.'" We thought these verses were so hilarious taken out of context. So the next day in the cafeteria, Erin ate a mouthful of food, smeared her mouth with her sleeve, and stated, "I've done nothing wrong!" Oh my, I have gotten so many laughs over that memory throughout the years. Then, when I was preparing for this study, Erin's verse came to mind. The passage actually starts, "This is the way of an adulteress . . ." As it turns out, the unrighteous woman who uttered those words was the same woman who was dressed like a prostitute! How often we women do or say something that could be harmful to another and without a thought for our actions, quickly dismissing it as "I have done nothing wrong." We might not use the NIV translation, but I can imagine the words "Whatever," "Big deal," or "So what?" What we have to realize is our words, actions, and wardrobes are a big deal. The memory is still funny to me, but now I carefully consider the harm I can cause another by acting or dressing inappropriately. Let's not be flippant and disregarding like the adulteress, but instead take on great responsibility in carrying out God's standard.

Now, bring the fattened calf and kill it. Let's feast and celebrate!

1. Can you think of a time in your life when you couldn't have cared less about your actions or what consequences they caused?

....

....

I sure can! Do you remember the story I shared about the time I modeled lingerie? I knew some people would make a fuss over it, but I didn't care what they thought. I was fine with it, and I felt they were judgmental legalists anyway. Looking back, had my heart been right with God, I would've seen their thoughts and opinions were completely justifiable. As much as I wanted to wipe my mouth and say, "I've done nothing wrong," I couldn't . . . because I *was* wrong. I thank God for being so patient with me. I was a self-righteous mess for many years. Praise God for His love and patience with me!

2. What are some of today's popular clothing labels that have a negative connotation?

....

....

3. What are some character labels that can be attributed to us based on our dress, whether those traits are true or not?

....

....

Verse Memorization: Proverbs 22:1

A good name is more desirable than great riches;
to be esteemed is better than silver or gold.

Signed: _____ Date: _____

Lord, thank You for Your Word. Thank You for teaching us how we should clothe ourselves. Give us wisdom about our clothing choices and the courage to follow through according to Your will as You guide us through the process of modeling modesty. In Jesus' name, amen.

—Rachel

Chapter Five

Fashioned to Be Feminine

Photo by Shane Greene

Hayden

Age: 15
State: North Carolina
Interests: skateboarding, guitar, piano, soccer, The Beatles, snowboarding
Future ambition: guitarist

he says . . .

As a teenager, I am immediately affected by the way a girl dresses. Of course, it also tells me numerous things about the girl. I can see what kind of attention she wants, and it tells me a lot about what she must be like. A low-cut shirt and short skirt make me think, *Gee, I wonder how many guys she's been with this week?* It makes me think she's never gonna be in a relationship for real love or friendship; it's just for sex. That does not fly well with me. Plus, this rather immodest apparel makes her a target for the wrong kind of attention. In other words, she'll attract all the guys, but for all the wrong reasons.

In contrast, when I see a girl who chooses to dress with decency, I get the sense she is real; she is comfortable with herself and comfortable with who she is. She isn't looking for attention or trying to catch someone's eye; she's just being herself. To me, that's an attractive feature.

Whenever I have a girlfriend, I want her to be as modest as possible for two main reasons. First, if I'm dating a girl and she dresses immodestly, other guys are going to be looking at her in ways I most definitely don't approve of, and second, it's putting things in my head I shouldn't be thinking about. I, like any other guy, have this tendency, and it is only made worse by the immodestly dressed girls we see everywhere.

I am the eldest of four siblings. I have one brother and two sisters. Jeslea is thirteen, Ella is six, and I already care about how they dress. I am the first to tell them if something they wear is immodest or inappropriate because I don't want other guys checking out my sisters! It's quite simple, what you wear sends a message—either positive or negative—to anyone who sees you.

—Hayden

she says . . .

Several summers ago I was working as a high ropes course and climbing wall facilitator at Word of Life Island Youth Camp in

Schroon Lake, New York. I was still represented by modeling agencies around the world, but was taking some much needed time off from the industry.

As I worked high in the trees or running belay at the base of the wall, my legs, torso, and arms bulked up. I was gaining muscle mass, and it added inches to my frame. I was at youth camp, so I was nowhere near a scale or tape measure, but I knew I wasn't the same size I was weeks before in Miami. I didn't care much though. I was fuller for sure, but I am *female*. Our bodies grow and change, and it wasn't the first time my weight had fluctuated. I wasn't modeling full-time; I was ministering at youth camp. Also, I thought I would have time to get back to an acceptable working size after camp and before moving on to the next model hub.

But I started to see the financial consequences of taking time off; after all, I still had a car, gas expenses, and school debt. So when my agent in Miami called to book me on a TJ Maxx job in Boston, I was thankful.

Two days after the call, I was to fly to Boston from Albany. Not much time to lose weight, so I began to stress. I knew if the client paid for my flight and confirmed me for $2,500 day, they would not be happy if I didn't fit into their clothes. I also knew they were on a schedule to get the photos out to print, and it would be tough to do a re-shoot or get a replacement. But the worst of all scenarios I imagined had me reimbursing the client for the expenses of the shoot and being dropped by my agent. And who could've blamed them? After all, my composite card stated my measurements, and those measurements did not jive with reality.

What could I do? I'm not sure I got much sleep leading up to the day I left for Boston. But on my way to the airport, my good friend

Kyle handed me a slip of paper and on it was written Matthew 6:25: "Therefore I tell you, do not worry about your life, what you will eat or drink; or about your body, what you will wear. Is not life more important than food, and the body more important than clothes?" I cried when I read it. Could I trust God with my eternity, but not my circumstances?

I "had church" on the way to my booking; I turned it over to God. If I had to reimburse the client, God would provide. If my agency dropped me, I'd find another to represent me. I learned my identity was *in Christ*—*not* in a booking, an agent, or a paycheck.

When I arrived at my job, everyone said their hellos and sent me to the makeup chair. After an hour of hair and makeup, I had time to sit and read. I could tell the wardrobe stylist was scrambling, but that seemed normal. This was a significant shoot for POS (point of sale) posters for the stores. What I did not know was the wardrobe I was supposed to wear had not arrived, and no one could track it. Conversations between the art director and client became heated, and the blame-game as to who was at fault began. They finally decided they had to move to Plan B.

The client phoned a local TJ Maxx and had the store rush over the garments that were to be shot. However, the store didn't have the size 6 I knew wouldn't fit me, but a size 12 . . . in *every outfit*! It would have to work. Instead of the usual pinning and taping done to the already small clothes to make them "fit" the model, this time a seamstress was in order. They brought her in along with the product. I must have been about a size 8 or 10, so the clothes hung on me like a burlap sack! The seamstress rushed to work, pinning the garments, cutting, sewing, and tailoring them to fit *me*. Ask any model; this *never* happens! The whole time I was reciting the verse in my head, "Do not worry . . . about what you will wear." I felt as if God were giggling at the sight of it all.

The shoot was a success. The tailored clothes fit me perfectly. And because of the interruption, no one realized that my size would have been an issue. Sometimes I wonder *when* the original garments finally showed up and *where* God had been hiding them. "I needed clothes and you clothed me" (Matthew 25:36). Thank you, Jesus.

He says . . .

> So God created man in his own image, in the image of God he created him; male and female he created them.
>
> —GENESIS 1:27

God specifically designed woman to complement man. He knew Adam needed a helper, but not just any helper. Instead he would need a helper who would meet the needs another *man* couldn't possibly meet. Man would need a partner to have and to hold. She would have curves that would ignite his passions and have a womb to bear his children. She would be able to nurse her babies with her own milk. She would have smaller features and delicate skin. King Solomon describes the beauty of the female form in the Song of Solomon.

God knew women would suffer from their own unhealthy body images. That may be one of the reasons He gave us Song of Solomon. Historically, it's written by the Hebrew king to his newlywed wife, but it is also an allegory, a story that teaches the truths of God's love for His people. In other words, we can replace King Solomon's words to his bride as Christ's words to us, His daughters. "All beautiful you are, my darling; there is no flaw in you" (Song of Solomon 4:7).

It's difficult to see ourselves as physically flawless, especially if we've suffered from weight gain, excessive weight loss, scars, birthmarks, acne, and so on. I've battled with some of these issues myself, and God must continue to remind me I am made in His image and I am *beautiful* (Song of Solomon 1:15).

Throughout my career, my weight has fluctuated, but I had to learn it is typical of a female's body. It was difficult to bear because I'd been so thin my whole life. I was even taunted for being *too* skinny. But early on in my career, while living in New York City, I began to put on weight. My agency noticed and brought me in for review. I had just turned nineteen, and my body was changing. My hips widened, my thighs plumped up, and even my shoulders rounded out. I was a healthy size 8, but bigger than my agency liked.

The pressure to get back to my original size was overwhelming. Without saying it, my booker implied that I—by any means necessary—should slim down. Fortunately, that agency is now out of business.

When weight loss regimens didn't work, I joined an expensive gym in Union Square Park. I worked out every day, usually two to three hours a day. When those means didn't succeed, I began to cut calories, *drastically*. I ate seven hundred calories a day and burned off a thousand. My knees were going bad because of the added stress and strain, and my health began to decline. But all I could focus on was slimming down. Amazingly, my stubborn body was not cooperating, and weight loss wasn't happening fast enough. That's when I decided to purge.

Purging is a nice way of saying vomiting. I distinctly remember eating a piece of lettuce, then forcing myself to throw it up so as not to retain any of the calories. This dangerous process lasted for about three weeks. I was scared I had stooped to such a low. Why was I willing to physically and mentally destroy myself for someone else's pleasure?

Sitting on the bathroom floor after having purged once more, I cried out to God. I confessed I was out of control, and I needed to be rescued. Desperate to change my ways, I went to my agency for help. Instead, I was dropped. Only God could save me. I backed away from the industry altogether and welcomed my weight as it was. It saved my life. For two years, I battled evil, bulimic thoughts. "Just one time" and "only after dessert" are the types of phrases that rang in my ear. I struggled, but resisted the temptation.

After recovering from the mental anguish that bulimia creates, I was able to get my weight under control, but only for a short time. Five years later I was living and working in London and booked a fantastic job in Majorca, an island off the coast of Spain. This is an excerpt from a letter to my mother from that trip:

Saturday, June 27: Today has been one of the biggest nightmares I could have ever imagined. It hurts just as much to recall it and write it down as it did to experience it, but here goes: The client asked me to leave a few hours ago because he said my face is heavier than it was when I cast for the job. He said they booked me on the next flight back to London leaving at 5:50 p.m. (It's now 2:30 p.m.) When I tried to tell him my weight was the same as it was at the audition, he became aggressive and said I was being "lippy," and he just wanted me out of there! I don't know what I'm feeling at this stage. I'm hurt, disappointed, and lonely. I don't have anyone to fend for me. The agency is closed, I can't contact my booker—and what would I say anyway?

To top it off, I was witnessing to the makeup artist this morning and even now she is siding with them. I know I'm not thin and bony like the other model, Sandra, but I was told I was being booked because I'm sporty. They already asked if I would dive off of a 50-foot cliff. Seriously? I did that in Hawaii! (Ok, so it was about 35 feet, but what's the difference, of course I'd try it!) But let's face it . . . I'm a basketball player, swimmer, runner, and a woman . . . but I'm not a twig! Okay, I've got to settle down a bit, I'm getting too defensive. I guess I've always put up my dukes when I've gotten hurt, and Mom, this really hurts. At this point, I don't even want to stay here with these people. I just want to wake up from this nightmare and be back home in London.

Wow! Revisiting this stirs raw emotions in me. I remember crying over this and feeling so much shame. My body belongs to the Lord, who made me female—and all the highs and lows that sometimes come with being female. Fortunately, I'd made up my mind. I would not return to eating disorders. Instead, I turned to the Lord. "In my distress I called to the LORD; I cried to my God for help. From his temple he heard my voice; my cry came before him, into his ears" (Psalm 18:6). I found comfort in Him who *fashioned* me to be *feminine*.

Did you know . . . ?

- Forty percent of newly identified cases of anorexia are in girls 15–19 years old.
- Anorexia has the highest rate of mortality of any mental illness.
- Only 6 percent of people with bulimia receive mental health care.
- The peak onset of eating disorders occurs during puberty and the late teen/early adult years, but symptoms can occur as young as kindergarten.
- Eating disorders affect people from all walks of life, including young children, middle-aged women and men and individuals of all races and ethnicities.
- Although eating disorders are potentially lethal, they are treatable.[1]

If you or someone you know struggles with bulimia or anorexia nervosa, there is help available. Please reach out—"All beautiful you are, my darling; there is no flaw in you."

So . . . what do you say?

The standard of the supermodel has changed throughout the years. It began with the rise of the voluptuous Marilyn Monroe. Back then, thick hips and a large bust were considered perfection for the iconic woman. In the '60s the trend changed to the boyish, hip-less body style of models like Twiggy. In the '80s the term *supermodel* was introduced and with it, curvy, toned women like Cindy Crawford and Claudia Schiffer. But as the '90s approached, Kate Moss brought back the waif and ultra-thin models; flat chests and average heights were the trend. Today, a size 10–12 is considered plus-size in the modeling industry, but the average American woman is 5'4" and wears a size 14!

The point is, whether you're tall, thin, curvy, or bony, you're always going to compare yourself to someone else unless you embrace *who you are*. The only standard for greatness is to love yourself from the inside out!

1. These days, when I work out and focus on eating healthily, I refer to it as "temple maintenance." The Bible teaches if we are Christians, our bodies are God's temple (1 Corinthians 3:16). Knowing this, how do you think God expects you to care for His dwelling place?

....

....

2. Some suggest the greatest female figure in all of history was Marilyn Monroe, and she is reported to have been somewhere between a size 10 and 14 and standing 5'5". In your opinion, give examples of how society has recently dictated what a perfect body is supposed to look like?

....

....

....

3. A Barbie doll's body is so disproportionate, if scaled into real-life proportions, she would be 5'9" and measure 36"-18"-33". According to research by the University Central Hospital in Helsinki, Finland, she would lack the 17 to 22 percent of body fat required to menstruate or bear children.[2] Has that societal opinion of perfection influenced the way you see yourself?

....

....

....

....

4. Why do you think young woman are willing to sacrifice their lives in order to be thin?

....

....

....

5. Have you ever entertained that thought? If so when?

....

....

....

My Commitment:

Today, I commit to reach out for help if and when I begin to struggle with my weight. Before I turn to an eating disorder, I will turn to God and will seek guidance from a trusted adult before it's too late. (If you are struggling with an eating disorder now, please commit to getting help from a guidance counselor, parent, or other trusted adult immediately.)

Signed: _____ Date: _____

Verse Memorization: Song of Solomon 4:7

All beautiful you are, my darling; there is no flaw in you.

Signed: _____ Date: _____

Lord Jesus, You are the Creator of all things. You have created me in Your image and have called me beautiful. Please help me realize the value You place in me so I can value myself as You do. Forgive any wrongful acts I have done to myself and please keep me from future self-destruction. In Jesus' name, amen.

—Rachel

Chapter Six

Fashioned for a Frame

Photo by Sarah Beasley

Brandon

Age: 15
State: Arizona
Interests: martial arts, hunting, paintball
Future ambition: restaurateur

he says . . .

We are a masterpiece made by God. Men and women alike each have their own special design that includes their personalities, appearance, emotions, and so forth. But sadly, most times we don't realize it. We don't understand we are masterpieces made by the best Artist's hands. We struggle with the words that come out of other people's mouths that are hurtful. We struggle with the words that run through our heads that say we aren't pretty, we are too fat, or we are too skinny. It troubles us because we buy into those thoughts, and soon we start saying them about ourselves.

I have no doubt women struggle with this the most. It's unbelievable how many of them buy into everything negative said about them. It hurts me to see them try to "perfect" themselves. Now, it's to the point that every girl you see is wearing clothes that reveal way too much of the skin on her body. And why do girls wear that kind of clothing? One reason is to get attention from guys. The worst thing about it is that it works. When I go to school, I find so many girls revealing themselves. It's sad to say, but they do it in church, as well. And here I am, a Christian guy, trying to stay pure and move my eyes from it and struggling to stop the lust. Everywhere a guy goes, there is a girl wearing something revealing. We're fighting a war every day to keep the lustful thoughts out of our minds.

I am only one of many Christian guys who struggle with lust every day. High school can be a killer! I'd be a rich man if I had a penny for every time I saw a girl walk around revealing what should not be revealed. Of course I *am* attracted to girls walking around like that. It's a desire all men have, but it upsets me that women know this and, yet, they still take advantage of it! They know what we think, and they don't seem to care as long as they get the attention they want. To me, it takes a real man to turn his eyes away. It takes a real man to be pure, but it's so hard to do.

On the other hand, there are girls out there who do dress

modestly. I love those girls! Whether they realize it or not, they're saving us so much difficulty. In my opinion, these girls are secure and strong and don't need to reveal themselves to know they are attractive. They aren't lost, confused girls who use their bodies to seek out attention. I thank these girls because I want to look at their face and get to know who they *are*, not their legs or other body parts. These girls are amazing because they know who they are, and they know they are masterpieces made by God!

—Brandon

she says . . .

What is a *masterpiece*? In a word, a masterpiece is an exceptional work of art. I love art. I studied it with a professional instructor for eight years and have won many awards with my works. Upon finishing a piece, it's important to frame it properly. If the frame overpowers the work, it distracts from its beauty. If it is too simple, it doesn't complement it properly. A good frame should always draw one into the artwork itself. The same principle applies to us as we attempt to add or take away from God's work. We are *His* masterpieces, and the way we adorn ourselves is the frame. Ephesians 2:10 says, "For we are God's masterpiece. He has created us anew in Christ" (NLT). Once upon a time, God fashioned you. Imagine Him excited at the thought of creating you and rushing to paint you into existence because He could not wait to see and appreciate the finished work. His work. And you're not just another piece in His collection: you're His *masterpiece*. Priceless. He handles you with great care, knowing your value. But to *this* masterpiece, unlike a canvas, he gives free will. Will you utilize it and realize your full worth? You have two choices: either to emanate beauty from within and adorn and frame yourself to please the artist, or wear the gaudiest frame possible, cheapening and weakening your appeal and drawing attention away from the Master's work. You see, the artwork's value never changes. It's still priceless to the Artist. But oh, if only the *masterpiece* could see itself the way He does.

In this chapter, we will address the specifics for a modest wardrobe from the waist down. Remember, these are not rules, only guidelines I use for myself. These are my recommendations, and just like our chapter for waist-up modesty, each of these is reliable and works with a *moving* body. And if we have to buy a bigger size, it's no big deal (no pun intended).

(You may need to speak with your parents about any reservations they have on these guidelines and, ultimately, the decision is theirs. Please respect and adhere to their wishes.)

UNDERWEAR: Yes, we're going there! Just like with bras, pants and shorts shouldn't be so tight we can see the outline of your underwear. We've all seen ugly panty lines but hopefully not in our own mirrors. It's as simple as making sure your underwear is fitted properly. If you're wearing "old drawers" (as my granny used to call them), it's time to go shopping! If they're too tight, not only will they be uncomfortable, they will squeeze and squish you into a panty line exhibition. If they're too loose from washing machine wear, they'll get bunchy. And no one wants to see your bunchy drawers!

Also, it's important to have flesh-colored underwear that matches your skin tone. A colored or textured undergarment under light-colored clothing is noticeable, so even though your days-of-the-week panties are cute, save them for your jeans. Even stark white undergarments can be visible under white pants, shorts, or skirts.

Not only should your underwear fit properly and be flesh-toned, the type of underwear you wear is important. Believe it or not, there is a place for granny panties. Many garments in my closet are white or light-colored and require a full-coverage panty. That means it is wide in the hip and covers under your cheeks. They're to be formfitting, so there will be no panty lines. Pantyhose will serve the same purpose. Some women substitute a thong in this case, but even they can show lines. So, while we're on the subject, let's discuss thongs.

Personally, I'm not a fan because they drive me crazy. I know one has to get used to them, but I can't stand waiting to get used to a string up my rear end. Another model friend of mine shares the same sentiment, and we always laugh about it. Either way, just be sure to remember underwear should never be considered outerwear and that includes panties—thongs or not—sneaking up above the top of your jeans. And please don't be peer pressured into wearing what your friends think you ought to wear under your clothes. It's a personal preference, whether you're a fan of granny panties, boy shorts, hipsters, bikini briefs, or thongs . . . just wear something.

PANTS AND SHORTS: These should not be too tight in the hip or thigh. To test this, see if you have horizontal lines in the fabric across the front of your shorts or pants. If you do, it means the fabric is being pulled to cover more rear than the size allows. It may be you've simply outgrown them. This can usually be remedied by going up a size. If going up a size or two makes them bigger in the waist, have them altered, wear a belt, or maybe opt for a different style that better fits your beautiful shape. With jeans, the wash may have "whiskering," which makes them appear to have these lines even if they're not too tight. It's just a trend and it's fine, as long as they're not actually too tight.

Something else to consider: I have a habit of putting my hands in my pockets and have noticed my pants weren't too tight until I did. That's not to say you can't use your pockets, just be aware of this if your pants are slim-fitting.

Lately I've seen the trend veer toward tight-fitting, or even skintight. It's possible to stay in style without being immodest. I love my skinny jeans because they're flattering and trendy. But skinny jeans don't have to mean skintight jeans. There is a difference. Mine are slim-fitted and tapered to my legs, not painted on them. A useful tip for me is to stand straight and pinch the fabric on my thigh and see if it stays. If it maintains some remnant of the bowed, pinched shape, they're fitted but still modest. If it snaps back (or the jeans are so snug I can't even pinch them), they're too tight.

Fingertip length is a standard I adopted in college and have used it ever since. Stand with your arms straight down to your side and place your hands on your thighs. Where your longest finger touches is the shortest length your shorts should be without baring too much when you sit or cross your legs. It's all about being able to move in different positions without having to constantly readjust.

DRESSES AND SKIRTS: Dress tops should follow the same guidelines as shirts. Neither should be made with a fabric too sheer or clingy. If they are, resolve not to wear them without a slip. It may be necessary to have long slips and short slips in white, black, and nude. If your garment is too sheer, the slip will serve as a lining. If it's too clingy, the slip will separate you from the garment. I had always thought slips were old-fashioned until I began working with Meg, a fashion client who expected me to bring them on every booking. What a difference it made in some of the clothes! And it expanded my options, allowing me to wear outfits I thought I couldn't.

Slits in skirts and dresses can also be alluring to guys, inviting them to finish the picture. A back-split may be okay, as long as it doesn't provide visual access higher than a few inches above the knee. Also, if the skirt curves too much under your rear, it's probably too tight.

Length is simple when it comes to skirts and dresses. To be modest, they shouldn't be any shorter than four fingers above the top of the knee, while standing. It will rise when you sit, so remember to keep your legs together.

SWIMSUITS: Is it possible to wear a modest two-piece bathing suit? Yes, but it's tricky. If the swimsuit is at least three finger-widths thick on the hips and covers your bottom and cleavage entirely, I would think it is modest. One-piece suits obviously cover more, but I have a hard time finding ones that fit me properly with my long torso and slim shape. Also note, a one-piece doesn't guarantee modesty. If it has a plunging neckline or Rio-cut back, it can actually be racier than a bikini. For me, because of my long frame, a tankini works perfectly. I am able to swim, play volleyball and football, or jog on the beach comfortably while still maintaining modesty.

Sometimes swimsuit straps can get stretched out and can constantly fall off your shoulder. They can be taken up or the suit can be retired altogether. Also, if the suit has lost its elasticity, it's time to shop for a new one.

Make sure the suit is thick enough to cover you on top and bottom. A well-lined suit is a must, especially if it's white. If there is any question about it, test it in the shower first.

One final thought on swimsuits: Be careful to wear your suit only at the pool or beach. Many times on vacation I'll notice girls running up the stairs to their hotel room or hanging out in the lobby in their bathing suits. An easy fix is to put on a cute cover-up, sarong, wrap, or even a pair of coordinating shorts before leaving the swimming area. It's both tasteful and fashionable.

CHEERLEADING, CROSS COUNTRY/TRACK, CREW, AND OTHER UNIFORMS: If you're on a team that has a less-than-modest uniform, you may or may not have much choice about wearing it. Usually it depends on the coach. I have seen cheerleaders wear coordinating, slim-fitting, warmup pants or leggings under their skirts without any issues from leadership. I was a cheerleader, and I know skirt length is sometimes thought of as a safety issue when girls are being basket-tossed into the air. But consider leggings or warmup pants under your uniform while wearing it to school on game day. You can easily slip them off for the pep rally and game.

Cross country or track shorts can be paired with bike shorts. A girl on a crew team whose uniform for competitions is a tight-fitting spandex suit can have a cover-up ready for when she steps out of her watercraft. Just because she wears it in the boat doesn't mean she has to wear it everywhere else.

Integrity, decency, and modesty are not virtues that should

be tossed aside when it doesn't seem convenient. Victory for your purity is more important than the victory of a thousand sports championships.

I know it might be easy to get discouraged or annoyed at these suggestions, but keep in mind I gave you an exhaustive list of options. I tried to cover everything I could think of, so you wouldn't have to. Once you have the guidelines down, you are free to express your individuality and shop till you drop. The standards don't change, only the styles. But no matter the style or latest trend, it's never fashionable to forfeit a beautiful work of art for a gaudy frame. You are God's masterpiece, and He is pleased with His work. Frame yourself accordingly!

He says . . .

For you created my inmost being; you knit me together in my mother's womb. I praise you because I am fearfully and wonderfully made; your works are wonderful, I know that full well.

—PSALM 139:13–14

I didn't always think of myself as "wonderfully made." Typical? Yes. But wonderful? No. I was a gangly child with extra-long limbs. Second tallest in my sixth-grade class, including the boys. My knees were knobby and huge. In fact, I had a defect in my knees called Osgood-Schlatter Disease. It's what happens when one's thigh and shinbones grow too fast for the rest of the body and play tug-of-war on the knees. The kneecap exhibits excess bone growth and a visible lump that is terribly painful. Because of this I wore a brace on my right leg to school. As if that weren't humiliating enough, I weighed 87 pounds and was 5'7". I had numerous nicknames, including Beanpole and Toothpick.

Couple my stick figure and knee issues with a bad perm and you can guess I didn't start off "model material." My parents couldn't afford the latest trends, so I had to make do with what I had. Then there was puberty. My skin stayed broken-out, and I thought I'd never outgrow it. Oh, and did I mention I also had to wear glasses, and my two front teeth overlapped one another? I needed braces for a while but didn't get them until seventh grade.

When I did finally get braces, I attracted new nicknames; words like *metal-mouth*, *iron-jaws*, and *brace-face* still ring in my ears. Those were painful and emotional years. Wonderfully made? You'd have been hard-pressed to convince me of this back then.

I say all of this so you will understand that I know what it means to suffer from self-esteem issues. I suppose God allowed me to go through that period of my life so I could relate to the many of you who experience it now.

David wrote heartfelt words to God in Psalm 139. It focuses on God's omniscience (His knowledge of all things), His omnipresence (His presence in all places), and His omnipotence, (He can do anything). It's important for us to realize God possesses all of these things and we have none of them. God knew I would deal with body image issues (omniscience), but He also knew He would be with me through it (omnipresence) and He could lead me out of it (omnipotence). It wasn't that He took away what I considered were my imperfections. I would struggle with these issues, along with my weight, throughout my career. But He could and would lead me out of the unhealthy self-image I had adopted. Until I accepted His creation as a masterpiece, I dealt with the painful blows of the modeling industry. Too fat, too tanned, too pale, bad skin. My bookers should have just said, "too ugly" . . . because that's how I felt.

One year, while working in Miami, I began dealing with a chronic skin condition called *rosacea*. A dermatologist put me on a prescription topical facial cream, but it didn't work. I changed my diet, cleaned my face with mild solutions, and did my best to keep out of the sun—all to no avail. I was with the strongest agency on the beach, and they were concerned about this ongoing problem. They were hesitant to give me work, but I insisted it was clearing up. It wasn't.

I booked a job for a Swedish magazine. It was one of those "this doesn't feel like a job" jobs. It was about spa treatments. In one shot, my toes were soaking in warm water seeping in aromatic flowers, in another I was pretending to sleep as I lounged poolside, and my favorite, for one I spent the afternoon soaking in the hot tub dotted with candles. It was relaxing and beautiful, and I found it hard to imagine I was getting paid $187.50 an hour to shoot it.

A few days later my agent called me in. I knew this was trouble. It meant they wanted to see improvements in my skin or they wanted to measure me. Either way, I was in for it. My blood pressure shot up. I cleaned my skin carefully and went in to see him.

He was just as busy as ever, taking phone calls and calling across the room to other bookers about castings and models. I could see work was abundant; I just wasn't getting much of it. He turned and examined me carefully. As empathetically as he could, he explained that the Swedish client refused to pay me. "They're claiming the film is worthless because of your skin, and this is unacceptable." The words *mortified* and *embarrassed* aren't even strong enough to describe my feelings at that moment. I didn't provide an excuse; I just agreed it was unacceptable. He dismissed me and I left. Before I could get into the elevator, tears welled up in my eyes. My insides were screaming at God and questioning, *Why? Why is this happening? Why do I have to deal with something I can't even control?* I went home to my roommates, Stephanie, a fellow model, and Heather, a professional photographer. They both flooded me with compassion. They knew my struggle, and like always, they knelt and prayed with and for me. The next day Stephanie confided in me that she, too, had dealt with skin issues, and in time God healed her. It was hard to imagine, because her skin was so radiant and flawless. "It wasn't always this way," she said, "but after battling years of acne, I prayed God would heal my skin, and He did." So we began to pray if it were His will, He would heal *my* skin.

God cares about all aspects of our lives. Not just the major issues, even though this *was* a major issue to me. He wants us to turn to Him in our need—whether it's for favorable results for a medical test, or a good grade on a math test. He wanted me to run to Him, turn it over to Him, and trust Him with the answer. He did heal me. But if He hadn't, I had come to the place where I could trust Him. I made up my mind that if He wanted me to pursue modeling, He would have to clear up my skin. I chose to follow God's will for my life, whatever that looked like. I also discovered that my identity was not in what I saw in the mirror; it was in Christ. He made me just as I am. I am still tall and skinny, I still wear glasses when I read, I still break out, and I still have bumps on my knees. But I—like you—am *wonderfully* made.

So . . . what do you say?

One afternoon my husband and I went to grab a snack at the local Sonic restaurant. We had already placed our order from inside our car. We were paying with cash, and we waited for someone to bring our order. Before long, a teenage girl roller-bladed up to our car, and my husband put his hand out of the window to pay for our meal. Just then his head snapped forward to avoid eye contact with the young woman. This, of course, got my attention, and I craned my neck to see what the fuss was about. As I anticipated, I observed the girl wore extremely short shorts that barely covered her rear. What I also noticed was that she looked a lot like me growing up: a cute girl plagued by acne. I knew my husband would normally look away to avoid the short shorts image, but I assumed that most guys would be so distracted by her poor skin that they wouldn't be looking at her body.

So I asked him. His answer shocked me but helped me understand the male brain. He stated simply, "Rachel, this is a real issue with men. Here's the deal—*we're not looking at their faces.*" Oooooooh. I had never thought of it that way before.

It doesn't matter if a girl doesn't think she's pretty enough or skinny enough. Too much skin, and a man can't get past the immodesty to notice the *rest* of a woman. That was ground-breaking for me. I thanked him for his honesty. It pains me that decent, solid Christian guys have to deal with this. It pains me that my husband has to deal with this. Theologian and pastor Al Mohler once stated regarding the temptations of immodesty, "If he's breathing, he's struggling."

1. Have you ever dealt with the notion that modesty doesn't apply to your life for whatever reason? Not pretty enough, not skinny enough, not cute enough for it to matter? If so, how does this story speak to you?

....

....

....

2. Have you ever felt—or do you now feel—like you can relate to my memory as a sixth grader?

....

....

If you have, you're not alone. As you've read, I have walked in your shoes. I know it's painful, but God loves you so much, and you *are* "wonderfully made." You are dear to Him and a great work of art! You have been touched by and created by the Master's hand, and no one's opinion of you negates that.

Years ago I represented North Carolina in the Miss Teen USA pageant. It was televised on CBS and had 200 million international viewers. When I made the top 12, Dick Clark brought me out for my onstage interview. He asked about my adolescent years as an "ugly duckling" and what advice I would give to other girls who felt the same way. My answer then is the same as it is today: "God is not finished with you yet."

Whether you feel like it or not, you are a beautiful swan.

This was in beautiful Charleston, South Carolina. Minimal make-up and tousled hair suits a simple shirtdress.

Hyde Park, London, England. It was my job to wrangle these three little dogs to face the camera. They had their own make-up artist that brushed and powdered them with talcum powder regularly.

Messages can easily be sent with nothing more than the eyes. Let your heart and eyes send pure messages, not impure ones.

This was for a wild hair show in London. After this shoot I went home on the Tube (the London subway system) like this. I think I scared people.

Photo by Rob Lang

(left) I love feminine details like capped sleeves and capris. Also, whites and off-whites are colors that represent purity and tranquility.

(below) Hats are great accessories, but the bold eye make-up steals this shot. If you do wear more on your eyes, go natural on the lips, and vice versa.

Photo by Mark Hanson for SeZen Magazine

(above) This was shot as a storm was approaching on Miami Beach. The photographer is a Christian friend of mine and we were praising the Lord together. She caught me in the act on camera.

(right) This was shot as the sun was setting in Miami Beach. Natural beach-wavy hair and simple make-up is my day-to-day uniform.

More of a high-glam shot, this one is a great example of layering and accessorizing.

Photo by Shane Greene

(right) Pearls are a delicate touch, even to this high-fashion ripped cloth dress.

(below) Wide-brimmed hats are more sophisticated than shorter brims. That's why this one was chosen for the Furnitureland South ad.

bring your style home.

FURNITURELAND SOUTH

Your Personal Guide to Shopping the World's Largest Home Furnishings Showplace

my time.
my place.
my self.

skirt also in petite & tall

Loved this skirt. I shot this for *Soft Surroundings* in gorgeous Santa Barbara, California. Modest and beautiful.

(above) It takes a team to pull off a successful photo shoot. This was for a golf company in Wilmington, NC.

(right) Shot in Boston, Massachusetts, this was one of my first Greg Norman bookings.

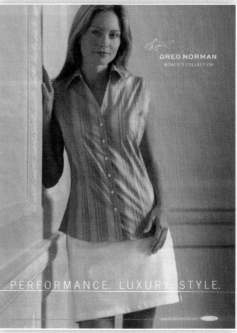

GREG NORMAN
WOMEN'S COLLECTION

PERFORMANCE. LUXURY. STYLE.

GREG NORMAN
WOMEN'S COLLECTION

PERFORMANCE. LUXURY. STYLE.

Photo by Michelle Joyce for Greg Norman Golf, Reebok

The wardrobe stylist decided to flip the collar on this one to show the detail underneath. Also, it elongates the neck. Just make sure that you tip the ends down, or you'll look too space age.

This is the *Aladdin*, the yacht we shot on in Jordan. The mountains in the background are on the coast of Israel. (Chapter 1)

Taking a break while shooting in Egypt, I watched this lady bake fresh bread.

(above) Started shooting just after 4:00 a.m. in the British Virgin Islands. This was in Virgin Gorda.

(left) Backstage for the Carolina Herrera Fashion show. Monochromatic dressing makes you look long and lean.

Shooting bareback on a white Arabian horse at sunset in Marrakesh, Morocco.

On this job, I woke up one morning to do my quiet time and read about Paul getting ship-wrecked right on this tiny island where I was shooting . . . Malta. These were some of my "heavier" days (chapter 5). The horse—unlike my agent—didn't seem to mind though.

(above left) Models always shoot winter clothes in summer and summer in winter. This was a hot day in Maine for *Cabela's* Catalog.

(above right) Since I couldn't get the dress wet I decided to change clothes once I got out onto the Mangroves. It was fun until tons of crabs started crawling all over me! I panicked and began laughing and screaming along with the all-women crew.

This is the Swedish magazine spa shoot I did in Miami that I didn't get paid for because my skin wasn't perfect (chapter 6).

I have a small foot in comparison to my height, so I hardly ever fit the shoes for a shoot. They would have had to re-touch the space between my heel and the back of the shoe!

Most times, the clothes on a shoot are too big for the models, so the wardrobe stylist has to make them appear to fit. Lots of clipping and pinning was needed to make this European shoot a success.

(above left) A shoot with my husband for the Biltmore Estate in Asheville, North Carolina.

(above right) In the make-up chair for Wella.

rachel and daryl 04.01.06
pleasant garden, nc

The best photo shoot ever—my
wedding day—published in
Weddings Unveiled magazine.

Hopefully, you won't be like me and take years to realize it. Let your identity be found in God, not in the mirror.

3. Have you ever been—or are you now—the girl who pokes fun at or uses cruel nicknames for others because of their appearance?

....

....

....

If you are that girl, keep in mind "wonderfully made" also applies to her. You are in a great position to show God's love for her by befriending her and taking up for her. Jesus spoke these words in Matthew 25:40: "The King will reply, 'I tell you the truth, whatever you did for one of the least of these brothers of mine, you did for me.'" We will be judged by our actions, not just our intentions.

Verse Memorization: Psalm 139:13–14

For you created my inmost being;
    you knit me together in my mother's womb.
I praise you because I am fearfully and wonderfully made;
    your works are wonderful,
    I know that full well.

Signed: _____ Date: _____

Lord Jesus, all of us at one time or another have struggled with self-image. We are guilty of comparing ourselves to what we see in the media. Help us realize that it is You who created this masterpiece. You have given us free will to frame ourselves in how we dress, so, Lord, please find us faithful. We love You, Lord. In Jesus' name, amen.

—Rachel

Chapter Seven

Fashioned to Bear Fruit

Photo by Zoe Zen

Tré
Age: 14
State: Tennessee
Interests: basketball, Tae Kwon Do, acting, reading
Future ambition: actor

he says . . .

When I see a girl dressed inappropriately, I can get carried away with my thoughts. But it doesn't take long for me to remember my thoughts can become words and my words can become actions. Because abstinence is what I believe in, I have to control what I think or feel when I see a girl wearing a low-cut top, short shorts, or a miniskirt.

Once I took out a girl who dressed inappropriately. During the date we kissed. Later I realized that with her inappropriate appearance came my inappropriate behavior, and I knew I couldn't get further involved with her. The temptation would just be too much.

I have come to the conclusion that girls who dress immodestly don't really feel good about themselves. Maybe some of them have problems at home that make them feel that dressing that way is the best way to get attention, or to feel loved or beautiful they should reveal their bodies. It confuses me because I can't imagine my mom letting my sister out of the house with her chest showing or wearing short shorts or revealing skirts.

I'm learning to have the spiritual fruit of self-control; my parents have taught me its importance from a young age. We always go to church, and I'm learning to renew my mind. I read my Bible, and it helps me to remember how God wants me to act, but I am still guilty of glancing at times because it's difficult not to. I think guys look at girls because it's natural, but I must admit my thoughts are completely different when I see a girl dressed modestly.

One thing I know: I *won't* marry a girl who dresses sexy in public, for the world to see. I just feel other guys will struggle with the same thoughts I have. But maybe they won't have self-control.

—Tré

she says . . .

Not long after I leased an apartment in New York City, my agent asked me to go on a "request casting" for a popular body wash campaign. A request casting means it is closed to other models and only requested models can audition. My chances are always better when I have been preselected, and it didn't hurt that it paid somewhere in the neighborhood of $40,000 for the job. There was just one catch. I would be in the shower, and although no nudity would be seen for the ad and commercial spot, I would have to be naked while it was being shot. The crew wanted to be sure underwear or a swimsuit wouldn't interfere with the filming of a bare back, thigh, or stomach. Let me be clear: this was not a closed set. And there are no less than thirty to sixty men and women on a commercial shoot. Trust me, I didn't have to think this through. The answer was no.

In another city I was asked about modeling in a similar situation—a shoot for a high-end bathtub. The client requested, for a $6,000 day, that I be nude in the tub. Again, my nakedness would never show, but it would make the photographer's job easier. (I'm sure it would!) I was assured bubbles would be up to my chin, and I would be relaxed in the water. Then why couldn't I wear a strapless swimsuit in the tub? Once again, my answer was no.

While working in Greece, I shot for an editorial that put me in this same, all-too-familiar position. I was asked to get into my next outfit. We had been shooting on location and were now back at the studio. It had been a long day. A normal shooting day in the United States is eight hours. In Europe, there's no limit. This was one of those fourteen-hour-plus days. I was already tired, but I was about to get a wake-up call I will never forget.

The outfit was a pair of silver pants and a sheer white top. I took one look at the shirt and wondered where the rest of it was. Realizing I had received the total ensemble, I proceeded to the dressing room.

When I returned, the wardrobe stylist said she could see my bra through the top, and I should take it—my bra—off. Just to show her it was too sheer, I did. I went back into the dressing room and removed my bra. I peeked out to make sure the male photographer wasn't around, then exited the room. I knew for sure she would agree the shirt was entirely too sheer to be worn alone. Imagine my surprise when she loved the look and told me to go to the set! I didn't move and told her I would *not* wear it this way. She said in broken English, "Bra no good, but no bra, okay." Without saying another word, I turned and went back to my dressing area. I took the top off, hung it on its hanger, and carried it out to her. When she saw me, she yelled at me in half Greek, half English to put the top back on and get to the set. I shoved the wrinkled top into her hands and without thinking, replied emphatically, *"You* wear it!"

I was furious and unafraid of the stylist, and she knew it. As I gathered my things to leave, the British makeup artist intervened. "You can wear it with something underneath if it makes you more comfortable." The stylist left the room without a response and never returned. So, having made my point, I returned to the dressing room.

While I probably didn't bear the fruit of gentleness too well, my actions certainly defined faithfulness (to my values) and self-control (by not being persuaded). Sure, it would have been easier to go with the flow and shoot the top (sheer as it was) how they wanted it. And chances are, no one in America would have seen it. But my Father would have seen it. I heard once that character is who you are when no one is looking. In this case, we can add when no one from America is looking.

I have a tattoo the size of a dime on the inside of my right heel. It's an *ichthus*—commonly known as the "Jesus fish." It is a great witnessing tool, and it was on this shoot that the makeup artist asked if my tattoo means I'm a Pisces. *Yuck, no.* I told her I wasn't into horoscopes, and only the God of the Bible knows the future. I went on to explain that the fish represents Jesus, God's Son, and He is my Savior. We had some good talks throughout the day about my faith.

How wonderful, she got to see my faith in action! That's what bearing spiritual fruits are all about; they are the evidence of our faith. As a Christian I am supposed be different. That way people can see my faith in action and want to know what *makes* me different, what *makes* me more loving and full of joy, peace, patience, kindness, goodness, faithfulness, gentleness and self-control. I didn't go with the flow as others may have. And when I stood up for my morals, my faith proved itself true. The makeup artist saw something different that day—she saw fruit.

He says . . .

But the fruit of the Spirit is love, joy, peace, patience, kindness, goodness, faithfulness, gentleness and self-control.

—GALATIANS 5:22–23

The fruits of the Spirit are the evidence of God in our lives. As Christians, when others see us they should see the evidence of Christ living in us—our fruit. But like anything from God, the devil offers alternatives, things in opposition with the nature of God. "For the sinful nature desires what is contrary to the Spirit, and the Spirit what is contrary to the sinful nature. They are in conflict with each other, so that you do not do what you want" (Galatians 5:17).

I love this quote by St. Francis of Assisi: "Preach the Gospel at all times and when necessary use words."[1] This is a perfect example of what the apostle Paul means when he says that we are to bear fruit. We should never need to tell people how to be patient or kind; they should see examples in our behavior when they spend time with us. If we have to *tell* people what we're like, then maybe we aren't acting the way we think we are.

Last summer my son Jack wanted to plant a garden. Our neighbor was moving and had offered us the remains of their fertilizing compost. So my husband went to work tilling the ground, and he and my two boys planted various seeds. That summer we had an abundance of rain, and between that and the compost, the garden flourished. In no time, it was full of veggie-bearing plants. In fact, our cucumbers grew as big as two feet long! We couldn't eat them or even give them away fast enough. At some point, we realized the cucumbers, squash, and cantaloupes had taken over our backyard. But it was fun to care for them, and now we wish we had entered some of our overgrown fruits in the county fair.

The point I'm trying to make is this: we reaped cucumbers, squash, and cantaloupes because we planted (sowed) cucumber, squash, and cantaloupe seeds. Green beans or strawberries could have never grown from our garden no matter how many seeds we'd planted, because we didn't sow green bean or strawberry seeds. In the same way, we can't reap the fruits of the Spirit when we sow seeds that appeal to our sinful nature. In fact, we will reap the opposite, fruits of sin.

Paul states in Galatians 6:8 that when we sow to please the sinful nature, we reap destruction. We make an unwise choice, and we reap the ugly consequences of our decision. We reap what we sow. Unfortunately, I've allowed this cycle to play out in my life way too many times.

On the other hand, we reap a harvest full of spiritual fruits when we sow the seeds of Christ and His Word in our hearts. A seed is planted when we first hear about Jesus (1 Corinthians 3:5–7), the seed is watered by reading the Bible (Ephesians 5:26), and the result is a life of fruit—love, joy, peace, patience, kindness, goodness, faithfulness, gentleness and self control.

Have you wondered where modesty belongs in the fruits of the Spirit? I made a list of how it relates in my life:

LOVE: I choose to dress modestly, first and foremost, because I love Jesus. I know—based on Scripture—that how I dress matters to Him, so it matters to me.

JOY: Joy is not the same as happiness. Happiness fluctuates depending on our circumstances; joy is a constant. It makes me joyful to know I please the Lord when I dress in a way that honors Him.

PEACE: There is peace between my husband and me because I choose not to flaunt my body in front of other men. Likewise, I don't cause division in another marriage by inciting jealousy or lust. In the same way, there will be peace between your parents and you on the subject of modesty when you adhere to their guidelines without trying to push the envelope.

PATIENCE: I must have patience when shopping for appropriate clothes. Every time I speak on this subject, women tell me modest but fashionable clothing is not available in the stores. Though I admit it can be difficult and time-consuming to find, it is possible. I wear the same size many of the women in my audience wear and shop at the same trendy stores. If I can find things to wear (or layer), so can they—and you can too! It just takes a little patience.

KINDNESS: Second Timothy 2:24 tells us we should "be kind to everyone, able to teach, not resentful." I think it's interesting these three phrases appear together. When God first convicted me of my wardrobe choices, I was immovable, definitely not teachable. When my pastor brought it to my attention, I was resentful. I cannot be these things and still have the spiritual fruit of kindness.

GOODNESS: If we dress immodestly, knowing it has the potential to make guys stumble, goodness never follows. We show a disregard for the way God fashioned men. We know they are visual creatures while we tend to be more emotional. Goodness would never use this knowledge against them for our own selfish ambition or to be trendy or seen.

FAITHFULNESS: Faithfulness is an attribute that means "to follow through." We can be faithful by being modest when it isn't convenient or easy, when it's too hot, or when everyone else is wearing something different. Modesty is a lifestyle and a habit. Like any habit, the more consistent we are, the easier it is to be faithful.

GENTLENESS: "Instead, it should be that of your inner self, the unfading beauty of a gentle and quiet spirit, which is of great worth in God's sight" (1 Peter 3:4). Gentleness comes from within and is poured out when we place more emphasis on inner beauty than we do on outward appearance. Immodesty deters inner beauty from showing, because the attention is always focused on the physical, not the heart.

SELF-CONTROL: To dress and act modestly can take lots of self-control. But when we exercise self-control in our wardrobe choices and in how we act, it's easier for guys to maintain self-control when they see us. And the example I set is especially important because I live with three boys. Because I love them, I don't want them to struggle any more than they already do. Since God loves them much more than I ever could, imagine how He would feel if I rejected the opportunity to show them how a woman of God should dress.

Romans 8:9 reminds us if we know Christ personally, we do not have to be controlled by our sinful nature. There is freedom in living a life teeming with the fruits of the Spirit. And just like my family's overgrown garden, when there is an abundance of fruit, there is more than enough to share!

So . . . what do you say?

I've always enjoyed working in front of the camera. At this point in my modeling career it comes naturally, but that wasn't always the case. I had a lot to learn in the beginning. I had to learn the angles. I had to learn what the camera sees. For instance, when the photographer is shooting with a wide-angle lens, I know whatever is closest to the camera looks larger. If my legs are stretched out toward the camera, I know they will look longer, but my feet will look like skis! If I lean forward at my waist, my torso will appear longer. Because I am double-jointed, I have to make sure my arms don't look deformed at the elbows when they're stretched out straight. My shoulder closest to the camera should be lower than the back shoulder. If I'm looking away from the camera, I should never look so far off you see too much of the whites of my eyes. My hands also have their proper place. They can never block the product or my face. They shouldn't wrinkle the garment I'm wearing even if my hands are in pockets or on my hips. They must never look hard or clenched. Instead they should stay soft and relaxed. If my neck is turned, I stretch it out as much as possible, so it won't appear wrinkled or ropelike, I drop my shoulders low. And I always, *always* offer different facial expressions from one pose to the next. Lighting on the set is just as important, and a lot of consideration is put into it being right for the shot, so I need to be conscious of the light source and be sure not to obstruct it. If the camera misses a flash I say, "No flash," so the photographer can adjust.

All of these things should be done without my having to think about them. As a professional, my movements need to be natural and fluent. If I look stiff or calculated, I certainly won't look natural, and looking natural is the most important attribute of an experienced model. If I can work without having to take a lot of direction from the photographer, it makes his job easier and the shoot finishes more quickly, which saves the client money and eliminates the need for a re-shoot. My pay rate may be higher than a less experienced model's, but if the shoot is a success, the client will be happy and I'll most likely be called to work with him or her again in the future.

As a model, I have learned that *movement matters*. It is how an agency, photographer, or client can see what caliber of model is in front of them. And that experience will dictate my paycheck. As Christians, our movements are evidence of a fruit-filled life. The way we carry our bodies, sit, dance, run, and walk tells of our moral character and spiritual fruit. A woman can be covered from head to toe, but not be exhibiting modest movement.

Several years ago I was booked for a job in South Beach for a prominent magazine. In the picture, I was supposed to be a mannequin. I was still expected to model, but my gestures were to look stiff and my eyes glazed over. The makeup artist was going to make me shine like polished plastic. It was an entertaining proposition, and I was excited about the shoot. Unfortunately, after hair, makeup, and wardrobe, the art director had an additional, unscrupulous request. She brought in an actual mannequin as a prop and expected the two of us to relate in a way that I wasn't comfortable with. Some might suggest that I wouldn't really be doing anything wrong, because it was just a piece of plastic—but I knew the appearance of the gestures was sinful. So I protested. The client became angry and called my agent. It was the first time I walked off of a set. I changed out of my wardrobe and headed for the door. Immediately, the client intercepted me and offered a solution. Instead, they positioned me on the couch and placed the mannequin several feet away, behind the couch. In this instance, I was dressed modestly, but my actions (or movements) should I have waivered would have dishonored God as much as if I were dressed immodestly.

1. Movement is a matter of self-control, one of the fruits of the Spirit. We can allow our actions to be evidence of our faith or not. But one thing is certain, others *will* notice. What are some examples of dressing modestly, but acting immodestly?

....

....

2. Another fruit of the Spirit is faithfulness. Since the birth of
prostitution—the world's oldest profession—women who were dressed
immodestly or worshiped idols were known as women who were
unfaithful. In Scripture, Hosea's wife, Gomer (Hosea 1:2–3; 2:2–5);
King Ahab's wife, Jezebel (2 Kings 9:22); the prostitutes in the Proverbs
(7:6–21; 23:27–28); and the false prophetess Jezebel of Revelation
2:20 are examples of this nasty trend. Look up one of these women
and describe how she was unfaithful and to whom she was unfaithful.

....

....

....

....

3. Obviously immodesty and idolatry lack the evidence of the spiritual
fruit faithfulness. Our deeds reflect what we believe, as do our
wardrobes. Ask yourself: when others inspect me for fruit, what do they
see?

....

....

....

Verse Memorization: Galatians 5:22–23

But the fruit of the Spirit is love, joy, peace, patience, kindness, goodness, faithfulness, gentleness and self-control.

Signed: _____ Date: _____

Lord, Your word teaches that the fruits of the Spirit—love, joy, peace, patience, kindness, goodness, faithfulness, gentleness, and self control—should be evidenced in my life. Although I am a work in progress, help me to allow these fruits to ripen to bring glory to You. In Jesus' name, amen.

—Rachel

Fashioned to Follow Through

Photo by Edward Austin Bowden

Chase
Age: 17
State: Alaska
Interests: art, blogging, apologetics
Future ambition: pastor

he says . . .

As a Christian teenage guy, the most challenging temptation to battle is bridling the natural passions God has given us. Too often, the reality of this daily strife is overlooked, and young Christian men

97

succumb to sexual temptation. Losing a battle with sexual temptation does not have to end with broken physical boundaries. In fact, more often this struggle is a mental one.

For women, their clothing is a statement of individuality. Appearances are not everything, but a woman's image reflects what she thinks about herself, and I believe that most Christian guys would agree.

When a girl dresses immodestly, not only is she a stumbling block—an opportunity that could lead someone into sin—but also she is presenting herself as insecure. Most girls dress in revealing clothes because they want to get attention from guys. Few girls, especially Christians, would admit that their tops are too low or their skirts are too short. As with most sins, no one wants to receive the blame for causing another Christian to stumble. But, ladies, please consider your apparel, because when you are around guys, our eyes will look; how much skin we see is your decision.

On the other hand, a Christian girl who dresses modestly is not only setting a standard for herself, but also reflecting the God she represents. Guys know that a girl worth keeping is a girl who does not need his approval because she is content with herself. She does not need to be codependent on a boyfriend because she is totally dependent on Jesus Christ.

When I consider the ideal girl, I ask myself what my parents would say. Without question, my parents would disapprove of a girl who did not dress properly; instead, my parents would be more apt to encourage a relationship if she wore appropriate attire. Girls are not the only ones who think about a long-term relationship, and I am living proof! In Christian circles, girls are always told to marry godly guys, but godly husbands want God-fearing wives too.

Also, I believe that modesty goes beyond clothing. An image is unveiled in clothing that the attitude confirms. And good guys want a girl who is modest and humble at heart.

If you have a boyfriend, you will never know how much trouble you keep him out of if you make the choice to dress modestly. If you're single, then follow God's heart and obey His commandments on clothing. It may not be black and white, what to wear and what not to, but if you have to question whether or not it is appropriate, more than likely it is NOT. Please choose to dress modestly, not for myself, not for others, not even for yourself, but out of love and obedience to your Savior.

—Chase

she says . . .

It's important that we follow through with all that it means to be modest—not just in our choice of clothing at church, but also in our everyday lives.

Typically, when I think of the phrase *follow through*, I think of basketball. I started playing organized ball in the fifth grade. One of the first things I learned about shooting a basketball is how to follow through on my shot. It basically means to *finish what I started*. If I toss the ball randomly at the hoop, it may or may not go in the net. But if I aim well, calculate the distance, and follow through with the tips of my fingers, the chances increase that I'll score.

That same analogy applies to my modeling career. Sure, I have made a deliberate decision not to compromise on wardrobe as it applies to my career, but what about the other days, when I'm not working? How do I dress when I go to the mall, the pool, or a party? What about when I'm out of town, at the beach where no one knows me? If my wardrobe decisions on the set or at church don't translate into everyday life, then I am guilty of being a hypocrite—and that's worse than dressing immodestly (Revelation 3:15–16).

Earlier I gave you some examples of how we can reassess our closets, by making use of most items just by giving them new purposes or tweaking them. I'd like for us to spend this section expanding on that principle. This is where you can follow through on modeling modesty.

First, we should go through our closets and drawers. This is more fun to do with a friend or during a sleepover. It's good to get others' opinions and their ideas on how we can turn immodest items into modest ones.

Start with undergarments. Are there any that need to be replaced? Has your bra size changed? While you're at it, separate your whites and nudes from your brights and blacks. This way you can get the right color tone easily depending on your wardrobe for the day.

Next, go through your shorts. Try them on, and any that don't meet the fingertip-length rule or are too tight can be used as sleep clothes—specifically the soft, comfy ones. Tight-fitting workout pants can also be used as sleepwear. Other ideas?

....

....

....

Shirts are easy—it's just a matter of finding new uses for ones that are too tight, low cut, or cropped. Strapless or spaghetti-strap tops can be worn with a shrug, over or under another tank top, or under sweaters and blazers. Tops that are too tight can be used as sleepwear or as camisoles underneath other tops. Low-cut or cropped shirts need to have long-length tanks worn under them. Other ideas?

....

....

....

There's not much you can do to salvage jeans that are too tight, unless you wear long tops over them. And by long, I mean mid-thigh long. Other ideas?

....

....

....

For summer dresses that are too short, plan to wear them over capris, long shorts, or jeans. Wear coordinating tank tops under spaghetti-strap or low, V-neck dresses.

Other ideas?

....

....

....

You will probably find that as you reassess your wardrobe, most of your clothes can be kept but used differently. For the items that can't be adjusted, altered, or used in other ways, I challenge you—if it's okay with your parents—to donate them or throw them out. It's a small price to pay when you can invest in your reputation instead.

Making these changes begins with a change of heart, and then follow through with your actions. Begin to search out items at your favorite stores that meet modesty standards or can be layered, and you will soon find that it is easy to dress fashionably and maintain integrity through a modest wardrobe.

He says . . .

> Forgetting what is behind and straining toward what is ahead, I press on toward the goal to win the prize for which God has called me heavenward in Christ Jesus.
>
> —PHILIPPIANS 3:13–14

When the apostle Paul wrote this, he used language and metaphors that his readers were familiar with—Roman and Greek game terminology. Forgetting the past and *straining toward what is ahead—the goal, the prize.* The original Greek games, or what would become known as the Olympics, began in 776 BC in Greece. The Roman Coliseum, which provided the venue for fighting gladiators, was built in the first century. Both of these would be in operation on or about the time Paul wrote this letter. He knew that his readers would connect with this parallel. In the same way, Paul encourages twenty-first-century readers to *follow through.*

As a competitor, I can relate to this verse as well. Regardless of what happened in the first quarter, I can forget it and still do my best in the second, third, and fourth quarters. Forgetting what happens on the front nine, I get a chance to shoot for par on the back nine. The same is true in our day-to-day lives. No matter what negative choices you or I have made, we can still ask for forgiveness and move forward with better intentions and stronger convictions.

As I already stated, my clothing choices and movements have not always been modest, but it doesn't mean that I cannot begin anew today. The same is true for you. Poor reputations stem from poor choices. But thankfully, God is in the business of resurrecting, and if He can raise the dead, He can restore our reputations. *Forgetting what is behind* . . . Forgetting doesn't mean that we can't recall it. It means that we're not under the authority of it. It doesn't control who we are today, or who we will become tomorrow.

And straining toward what is ahead . . . Have you ever strained or worked so hard for something that you ignored the pain because the outcome was too important? When I was in the ninth grade, I was running the 300-meter hurdles for an all-conference track meet. Coming around the last bend of the track, I gave everything I had on the straightaway that was before me. I thought it was literally going to kill me, but somehow I found the strength to finish strong. *I followed through.* Strain toward what is ahead. None of us can change the past, but we can rewrite our present and redirect our future.

I'm sure King David didn't get up that fateful morning with the intentions of lusting after the bathing Bathsheba, sleeping with her, and then murdering her husband. But he did all of those things. Obviously he had become prideful and entitled. Seeing an undressed woman that didn't belong to him was the proverbial straw that broke the camel's back. David and Bathsheba both sinned, and they were both to blame. She could have chosen to be more discreet, or resisted his advances. Could he have resisted his urges? Of course, but he, like many Christian men, fell to lust and passion after viewing the tempting woman's body. He wasn't wicked; he was weak.

While I was studying the story of David and Bathsheba, and the role immodesty played in their downfall, I came across this anonymous article written by a Christian man. Here is a section of that article entitled "The Sin of Bathsheba—An Appeal to Christian Women by a Brother in Christ."

> You have no right to destroy by your careless dress, the brother for whom Christ died. You are bought with a price and you are not your own [1 Corinthians 6:20]. You are duty-bound to glorify God in your body—to clothe that body, not as you will but as God wills. And a little love for the souls of your brethren would remove forever from your heart the desire to dress as you please. . . . The perfectly obvious design of your beauty is to ravish and satisfy the heart of a man—but only one man, not every man.[1]

Many of us have made mistakes in our wardrobe choices, and many of us did so with the same intentions Bathsheba possibly had—to get the guy. Fortunately, we each get the opportunity to follow through by making changes that reflect God's heart. That may mean it's time to visit the closet and remove items that don't represent a moral Christian woman. Or it may mean that it's time for a visit to the mall to shop for some long-length tank tops and longer shorts. Or it could mean it's time for a sincere heart check.

That's what David did. He asked God to search his heart (Psalm 139:23), genuinely confessed his sin, sought forgiveness, and was restored. Was he perfect? No. But he was fashioned to follow through, and by God's grace, he did. What about you?

So . . . what do you say?

The Bible is quite clear on our responsibility as women for our clothing choices. As Nancy Leigh DeMoss explains, it often comes down to putting the interests of our Christian brothers ahead of our desire to be immodestly fashionable. She wrote, "It's a heart issue before it's a clothing issue." She went on to set this scenario:

> [Defrauding] means to create an expectation that you can't righteously fulfill; one who dresses in such a way that teases or tantalizes or tempts the men around her.
>
> So as a woman dresses or walks or conducts herself in such a way that says, "I'm available; here's my body. Here's an invitation; come to my party" and then she says, "I don't really want you at my party. I didn't mean it. . . . I don't want to get sexually involved. I just wanted to dress in such a way that I was sending you an invitation." . . . She defrauded that man. She created an expectation that she could not righteously fulfill.[2]

1. The power that comes with the knowledge of seduction can be deadly. Write out Matthew 26:41:

....

....

....

2. How does this verse apply to men who have to face the temptation of immodest women?

....

....

3. How does it apply to women who want to dress fashionably?

....

....

....

I know the temptations that come with wanting to dress in the latest trends regardless of the skirt length, but I also know that God changed my heart about it. He can change yours, too, if you'll permit Him. You've learned what it means to be modest in dress and actions, how immodesty affects men, and the ramifications it causes both historically and presently. As with all things spiritual, it comes down to a choice.

A girl should be two things: classy and fabulous!

—Coco Chanel[3]

Verse Memorization: Philippians 3:13–14

Forgetting what is behind and straining toward what is ahead, I press on toward the goal to win the prize for which God has called me heavenward in Christ Jesus.

Signed: _____ Date: _____

Lord, I pray for those reading these words, and know that for some this may seem like an improbable proposition. It was for me. Thank You for trading my selfish heart for one that wants only to glorify You in my actions and dress. Please summon the hearts of these readers to hear Your voice—the final authority on all things—and give them the courage to do Your will and follow through. In Jesus' name, amen.

—Rachel

Chapter Nine

Fashioned Forever

Ty
Age: 22
State: South Dakota
Interests: golf, cross country, track and field, piano, art, traveling
Future ambition: sports ministry

Photo by Rachel Lee Carter

he says . . .

"I am not letting you out of the house wearing that outfit." "Could you please put on a longer pair of shorts?" "You are not going to the party with that top on." Maybe you have heard this before from a parent, but ask yourself, "What is wrong with wearing a low-cut top or a pair of short shorts?"

While I am not a girl, I can imagine you must be frustrated and possibly confused with a modest dress code. You don't want to dress like your grandmother; yet, you are forbidden to wear the "cute" outfits in your closet. I think it is important for you to understand that what you wear really does matter, and there are hidden consequences for dressing outside of these lines.

From a guy's point of view, I have a greater respect for girls who respect themselves and show that by how they dress. In fact, I am more attracted to a girl who dresses modestly than to a girl who lets it all hang out. Unfortunately, our culture tells girls that in order to be beautiful, they must dress sexy and wear the latest fashion, when in reality, the most beautiful thing you can do is to be yourself and allow your personality to shine. Physical beauty is fleeting, but a beautiful personality will last forever.

It is also important to see the big picture and to understand the consequences of dressing immodestly. When girls dress in this way, it gives guys the impression that you want us to love you for how you look rather than for who you are. The trouble with this is that you will forever feel pressure to look good, not to mention the insecurities it will cause down the road when you feel you don't live up to a certain standard.

—Ty

she says . . .

All good photographers know that when they're shooting they need good light. The light source is possibly the most important feature of the photo shoot—more important than the model, in fact. Good lighting can make a tired model look radiant; a model with wrinkles, young again; and if the light is "blown out" enough, she can look angelic.

Miami, Florida, became a modeling hub in the 1980s. Every year from October to April, models come from all over to work for the thirty-something agencies represented there. Clients from every part of the globe come to shoot their spring and summer lines. Why? Because of the *light*. The sun is situated in such a place that you can begin working early in the morning until early in the evening with pristine light. The light is clear and intense, but not hazy. The only other place like it is Cape Town, South Africa—another modeling hub.

A typical day might start with hair and makeup at 5:45 a.m., so the shooting can begin at 7:00 a.m. Photo shoots start early so the crew can break for lunch while the sun is directly overhead, because when it's at that angle, the model gets shadows under her eyes from her lashes—this is *hard* light. After lunch, the sun has moved again, and it is at the right angle to light her face without shadows. A scrim (a kind of flattened white umbrella) is sometimes used to diffuse the brilliant rays.

Particularly in Miami, the light might be on the verge of blinding me, but it's all about what the camera sees. The camera is seeing flawless features. Not because I am flawless, but because the light is entering every possible crevice—scars, wrinkles, the dark circles under my eyes. But there is not only a light source but a "fill" light. This is light that is reflecting off of the sand under my feet, or a white foam core board just below me or to my right or left. Its job is to *fill in* every possible shadow that the light source might have missed. If you have great light, you don't need retouching. Notice all the makeup ads or commercials. They flood the model with light. And it's beautiful.

In the Bible, sin is often described as darkness. It can also be referred to as *lightlessness,* because it is the absence of light. One unfathomable attribute of heaven is that it has a constant source of light. Imagine—no shadows. Perfect light everywhere (Revelation 21:23; 22:5) without the need for a scrim or fill light.

We also read that we are "the light of the world" (Matthew 5:14), and we are to "reflect" Christ (2 Corinthians 3:18). It doesn't mean that we're flawless. It just means that we are to reflect the *light source.* Christ is the ultimate light source, and in His presence, it's easy to reflect Him. When we're following Him, by reading His Word and seeking His will, we are living in God's image, and people will notice that reflection.

When you've met those who love Jesus with their hearts, souls, minds, and strength, you know that they're reflecting the light source. And it's *beautiful.*

He says . . .

That if you confess with your mouth, "Jesus is Lord" and believe in your heart that God raised him from the dead, you will be saved.

—ROMANS 10:9

I grew up going to church and made a decision to be a Christian when I was seven years old. I was merely a church kid with morals, but looking back, I'm not convinced that I was what the Bible calls *saved*, or *born again*. Jesus taught that we're all born once physically, but in order to be alive spiritually, we must be born again (John 3).

In high school, I spent more time trying to blend into my friends' world than I did trying to stand out. I swore like they did. I laughed at and even told obscene jokes. I harassed unpopular kids. I had conflicts with other girls. And I gossiped, lied, and cheated occasionally on my homework. Schoolwork wasn't as much of a priority as cheerleading was. I almost always had a steady boyfriend, and often my identity was wrapped up in him and our impure relationship. Like most people I knew, I went to church. But I juggled being a "Christian" on Sunday or at youth camp, and disregarding the things of God the rest of the week. There was no evidence that I belonged to Jesus. I wasn't fooling anyone, except myself.

Many people believe that they will go to heaven when they die simply because they're a good person. But good compared to whom? Hitler? Billy Graham? The term *good* is relative. But just for argument's sake, let's say we *are* a good person, or at least our good works outweigh our bad. Now, imagine a huge scale—all our good works on the right and all our bad works (or sins) on the left. If the good outweighs the bad, we might conclude that we're safe. But the problem is that there's still bad on the left side of the scale. The sin hasn't been dealt with, and God is too holy to allow sin to dwell in heaven. In fact, Romans 3:23 reminds us that we are all sinners—no one is excluded.

The Bible states, "The wages of sin is death, but the gift of God is eternal life in Christ Jesus our Lord" (Romans 6:23). A wage is an earning. If we have a job, we're paid a wage. If the wages of sin is death, then death is what we have *earned* for being sinners. Even if we've sinned one time, the Bible says we're sinners and not fit for the kingdom of heaven. Here is the problem—we have to get rid of our sins, but we can't do it on our own.

In Hebrews 9:22, we read that "without the shedding of blood there is no forgiveness" of sin. This means that as sinners, we need bloodshed to forgive our sins. I can't die for you, because I'm a sinner. You can't die for yourself, because you're a sinner. We need a person who can shed blood and die who is *sinless* to pay the penalty for our sins. But the only One who is sinless is God.

In Jeremiah 10:10, the Bible teaches that God is eternal and can't die. So in order for us to have forgiveness for our sins, God had to make Himself into human form, so He *could* die. So He did. God came in bodily form: Jesus. Jesus was fully God and fully man (John 10:30). He was fully God to be sinless to pay the penalty and fully man (John 1:14; Luke 2:7) to be able to shed blood and die.

The second part of Romans 6:23 says, "The wages of sin is death, but the gift of God is eternal life in Christ Jesus our Lord." That's a big *but*! The writer, Paul, aptly uses the term *gift* because in order to *have* a gift, one must *receive* the gift. Someone can offer us a present, but if we don't receive it, it's not ours. That's why God doesn't force us to accept Him. It's our choice. He settled the issue of sin when He came to earth in the person of Jesus, God in bodily form; died on the cross; shed the only blood that could cover our sins; and then rose from the grave to end the curse of eternal hell for all who will receive Him as Lord. When we accept the gift of His sacrifice, we get to start over—we are given a new nature that is clean before God—and that's why Jesus called it being *born again* (John 3:5–7).

After graduating high school, I moved to New York. I was eighteen and had an apartment in Queens with three other girls. Eventually, I convinced myself out of pride that I didn't need to be in Queens but in Manhattan, where real models lived.

At first I thought I was living a life of freedom—doing anything I wished without having to report my activities to anyone or ask permission to do anything I wanted to do. I had my own downtown apartment in New York City; I was mingling with celebrities, going to parties and prime time sporting events.

I thought I had the world by the tail, but it had me. Everything on the outside looked fine, but on the inside I was miserable and empty. In the still of the night, my heart ached for a relationship with the Jesus that I learned about as a child. I remembered I had made that decision to follow Jesus years before, but my choices did not reflect that I was born again. I was full of pride. I was going to places I shouldn't have been going, doing things I shouldn't have been doing, with people I shouldn't have been with. My language was filthy, my wardrobe was degrading, my music was ungodly, and my relationships were toxic.

Out of curiosity, I began delving into new age religion. I was intrigued with my horoscope and other mysticisms. As harmless as I thought this was, it was extremely dangerous. The Bible warns us, "Let your astrologers come forward, those stargazers who make predictions month by month, let them save you from what is coming upon you. Surely they are like stubble; the fire will burn them up. They cannot even save themselves from the power of the flame" (Isaiah 47:13–14). The Bible says to "be self-controlled and alert. Your enemy the devil prowls around like a roaring lion looking for someone to devour" (1 Peter 5:8). Satan was having a field day with me. And just as he planned, I began to doubt the faith I was raised in.

God's love for me poured out as He intervened and began taking things out of my life that were separating me from Him. That's when I started gaining weight, bookings were few and far between, and my bank account began to dry up. Refusing to let God have His way, I went to work at a bar to make ends meet. Bulimia and exercise became routine.

But God wasn't finished with me. He wasn't going to leave me where I was. I met two Christian models who shared similar stories of running from or questioning God. Their transparency comforted me. They encouraged me to confess my doubts to God and tell Him I was searching for truth. I ached for what they had.

Desperate for more, I went to a popular Bible-believing church to get counsel from a pastor. I confessed everything. His words were nurturing as he steered me back to Scripture. Just as the two models had, he urged me to get honest with God.

It took getting honest with myself before I was able to get honest with God. I came to the place where I realized that I didn't deserve God's favor or His heaven. I read John 3 and Romans 6:23 over and over. I was a sinner and a hypocrite. But it was the best realization I could have had—after all, a person can't be found if she doesn't know she is lost. So, as a broken, humbled nineteen-year-old, I prayed to receive this gift of God—to be born again—and He changed the course of my life forever.

Jesus extends this invitation to you as well.

You may feel God tugging at your heart—that's His Holy Spirit. He loves you so much that He was willing to suffer and die to pay your sin debt, so you wouldn't have to.

In Romans 10:9, the Bible says that we should confess with our mouths, saying, "Jesus is Lord," and believe in our hearts. In other words, it's not just saying the words that saves you, but the attitude of your heart. Knowing this, you can simply pray as I did,

> Lord Jesus, I am a sinner and I need You. Please forgive me of my sins. I confess with my mouth and believe in my heart that You are Lord. I want Your gift of eternal life, and by faith I now receive this eternal gift. Thank You for loving me and for saving me just now. In Jesus name, amen.

If you meant that prayer, the Bible says that you can know that you have eternal life (1 John 5:13). And it is by "grace you have been saved, through faith" (Ephesians 2:8). That is what it truly means to be FASHIONed by FAITH . . . forever!

So . . . what do you say?

If you prayed to receive Christ, I hope that you will share that decision with someone—a church leader, friend, or parent. Paul stated in Romans 1:16 that he was not ashamed of the gospel of Jesus Christ. Girlfriend, I'm not either, and I hope you'll join me in voicing it with others.

> Today I, _____, confessed with my mouth and believe in my heart that Jesus is Lord. I trust in Him alone for my salvation. Today, _____, is my spiritual birthday! Witness: _____

Paul said, "So I strive always to keep my conscience clear before God and man" (Acts 24:16). With regard to modesty, do you have a clear conscience before God and others? It has taken some time, and this book outlines some of those struggles, but I can now say my conscience is clear. That is freedom. And that's why I wanted to share it with you. You too can be free of the comparisons, jealousy, blame, debate, and guilt. Becoming a modest-conscious model is one of the greatest decisions I ever made—now you can make a similar decision too.

Today I, _____, commit to a lifestyle and wardrobe of modesty to the best of my understanding. I will make the effort to shop and dress in a way that pleases the Lord. And I will allow Him to continue to refine my heart and permit others to hold me accountable.

Today's date: _____ Witness: _____

Lord, You know our hearts, and You know our deepest desires. Transform them both by the renewing of our minds. Help us to live a life pleasing to You in the area of modesty. In Jesus' name, amen.

—Rachel

Conclusion

One of your most powerful means of proclaiming Christ is through modest movements and wardrobe. You have the tools necessary to make the changes—in your heart and in your closet. The great theologian Oswald Chambers wrote, "His commands are difficult. But they become divinely easy once we obey."[1] I have found this profoundly true, especially on the issue of modesty. How else could I—a professional model, a clotheshorse, and a lover of fashion—become an advocate of the modesty movement if it weren't for God's work in me? I became teachable and eager to know the truth. And the truth set me free (John 8:32). I was set free from becoming a slave to this culture and its skin-baring trends. Free from believing the lies about weight. Free to find my identity in Christ instead of the mirror.

I have a steady self-respect and confidence about myself. Joy abounds.

I now have the knowledge of knowing that my modest actions and dress are pleasing to the Lord. I know that these decisions protect me from the wrong kind of attention. I know that it brings security to my husband. I prevent him and others from questioning my intentions. I know that other women don't have to worry about me appealing to their husbands' sexual natures. I am confident that my dress does not cause others to stumble. My conscience is clear before God and man.

I am valued for more than my body. I know that my attraction stems from the Lord within me, not the external that will soon fade. My worth is not based on my appearance—it is based on unfading beauty.

My actions and my wardrobe have the ability to point people to Jesus by making the gospel believable in me. I have noticeably been transformed by the renewing of my mind. I have a deeper walk and relationship with Christ, my Savior.

My wardrobe reflects humility, freedom, and purity.

I am fashioned by freedom, forgiveness, favor, and faithfulness. To be feminine, for a frame, to bear fruit, and to follow through, forever . . . I am fashioned by FAITH.

And so are you.

Fashioned by Faith
45-Day Bible Study

Chapter One: Fashioned by Freedom!

Day One
Read 1 Peter 3:4.

> *Instead, it should be that of your inner self, the unfading beauty of a gentle and quiet spirit, which is of great worth in God's sight.*

How does God define beauty?

....

....

What does it mean to have a gentle and quiet spirit?

....

....

Lord, teach me what it means to have Your unfading beauty and a gentle and quiet spirit. In Jesus' name, amen.

Day Two

Read the following verses:

> *I also want women to dress modestly, with decency and propri-*
> *ety, not with braided hair or gold or pearls or expensive clothes.*
> —1 Timothy 2:9

> *Your beauty should not come from outward adornment, such as*
> *braided hair and the wearing of gold jewelry and fine clothes.*
> —1 Peter 3:3

What do the words *modesty*, *decency*, and *propriety* mean to you? Look them up in a dictionary if you want to get an idea of their definitions.

....

....

....

....

Why does the writer Paul in 1 Timothy say these things are important for a woman of God?

....

....

Do you think God doesn't want us to braid our hair, wear beautiful jewelry, or have expensive clothes?

....

....

Lord, please help me to incorporate modesty, decency, and propriety into my daily attitude, speech, and wardrobe. In Jesus' name, amen.

Day Three

Reread 1 Peter 3:3.

Your beauty should not come from outward adornment, such as braided hair and the wearing of gold jewelry and fine clothes.

—1 Peter 3:3

If the apostle Peter is saying our beauty should not come from outward adornment, where is he suggesting it should come from?

....

....

....

Have you ever met a woman who, by the world's standards, is not physically attractive, but is enormously beautiful on the inside? Why do you think that is?

....

....

....

Lord Jesus, help me put more emphasis on what You consider beautiful. In Jesus' name, amen.

Day Four
Read Proverbs 11:22.

> *Like a gold ring in a pig's snout is a beautiful woman who shows*
> *no discretion.*

What does the word *discretion* mean to you?

....

....

Explain the symbolism of a gold ring in a pig's snout and a beautiful woman who lacks discretion.

....

....

....

Compare that illustration to something we see today in magazines or on TV.

....

....

....

Lord, teach me fully what it means to be a beautiful woman of discretion, and help me rely on You, the only One who can make me truly beautiful. In Jesus' name, amen.

Day Five
Read 1 Corinthians 12:23.

> *And the parts that we think are less honorable we treat with special honor. And the parts that are unpresentable are treated with special modesty.*

What is the Bible referring to when it says the "parts of the body that are unpresentable"?

....

....

What do you consider unpresentable?

....

....

Lord, help me recognize the parts of my body that should be treated with special modesty and have the courage to follow through in my dress. In Jesus' name, amen.

Chapter Two: Fashioned by Forgiveness

Day One
Read Proverbs 7:6–23.

> At the window of my house
> > I looked out through the lattice.
> I saw among the simple,
> > I noticed among the young men,
> > a youth who lacked judgment.
> He was going down the street near her corner,
> > walking along in the direction of her house
> at twilight, as the day was fading,
> > as the dark of night set in.

> Then out came a woman to meet him,
> > dressed like a prostitute and with crafty intent.
> (She is loud and defiant,
> > her feet never stay at home;
> now in the street, now in the squares,
> > at every corner she lurks.)
> She took hold of him and kissed him
> > and with a brazen face she said:

> "I have fellowship offerings at home;
> > today I fulfilled my vows.
> So I came out to meet you;
> > I looked for you and have found you!
> I have covered my bed

with colored linens from Egypt.
I have perfumed my bed
*   with myrrh, aloes and cinnamon.*
Come, let's drink deep of love till morning;
*   let's enjoy ourselves with love!*
My husband is not at home;
*   he has gone on a long journey.*
He took his purse filled with money
*   and will not be home till full moon."*

With persuasive words she led him astray;
*   she seduced him with her smooth talk.*
All at once he followed her
*   like an ox going to the slaughter,*
like a deer stepping into a noose
*   till an arrow pierces his liver,*
like a bird darting into a snare,
*   little knowing it will cost him his life.*

Why do you think the Bible purposely describes the adulterous woman's attire?

. . . .

. . . .

. . . .

Do you think her attire attracted this young man who lacked judgment?

. . . .

....

....

....

Father, open my eyes to see what You see, and equip me to be the young woman You created me to be. In Jesus' name, amen.

Day Two
Read Proverbs 7:24–27.

> *Now then, my sons, listen to me;*
> *pay attention to what I say.*
> *Do not let your heart turn to her ways*
> *or stray into her paths.*
> *Many are the victims she has brought down;*
> *her slain are a mighty throng.*
> *Her house is a highway to the grave,*
> *leading down to the chambers of death.*

Why does God warn young men against women like this?

. . . .

. . . .

If God were writing this about you and your choice of dress, would He have to warn young men about you?

. . . .

. . . .

There was once a time in my life when God would have warned young men about me. I praise Jesus He opened my eyes to this, and helped me to accept responsibility for it. If this is or has been you, you are not alone. It is why we have a Redeemer.

God, help me to not excuse what You call sin, and forgive me when I've put my will above Yours. Help me to be sensitive to Your voice in everything I do. In Jesus' name, amen.

Day Three

Read Proverbs 6:25.

> *Do not lust in your heart after her beauty*
> *or let her captivate you with her eyes.*

In your own words, define *lust*.

....

....

....

Is lust the guy's problem or does any responsibility fall on the girl who's dressed immodestly?

....

....

....

What does it mean to be a stumbling block?

....

....

....

Why is causing another to stumble important spiritually?

....

....

....

Lord, help me not to be a stumbling block for my brothers. In Jesus' name, amen.

Day Four

Read Job 31:1.

> *I made a covenant with my eyes*
> *not to look lustfully at a girl.*

What is a covenant? (Feel free to use a dictionary.)

....

....

Why did Job make a covenant with his eyes?

....

....

What are some things women lust after?

....

....

Lord, help me make a covenant not to lust after the things of this world. In Jesus' name, amen.

Day Five

Read 1 Corinthians 10:31–32.

> *So whether you eat or drink or whatever you do, do it all for the*
> *glory of God. Do not cause anyone to stumble, whether Jews,*
> *Greeks or the church of God.*

Note the phrase "whatever you do." Can how we dress fall into this
category? Of course! What are some ways we can give God the
glory?

....

....

....

....

What are some other ways, beyond the way we dress, that we can
cause others to stumble?

....

....

....

....

Lord, I know You care about my brothers in Christ as much as You care about me. Help me to see and understand the influence my wardrobe has on their spiritual growth . . . and my spiritual growth. Help me take my clothing choices seriously for all our sakes. In Jesus' name, amen.

Chapter Three: Fashioned for Favor

Day One
Read Ephesians 5:3.

> *But among you there must not be even a hint of sexual immorality,*
> *or of any kind of impurity, or of greed, because these are improper*
> *for God's holy people.*

What things or actions can be defined as a "hint of sexual immorality,"
or "any kind of impurity"?

....

....

....

Why does God say it's improper for His people?

....

....

Wearing immodest clothing such as cleavage-baring tops and
miniskirts could certainly be considered examples of "hinting at sexual
immorality." What other items in a wardrobe could do this?

....

Lord, help me to be found pure and not to defile myself by my thoughts, actions, or clothing choices. In Jesus' name, amen.

Day Two

Reread 1 Timothy 2:9.

> *I also want women to dress modestly, with decency and propriety,*
> *not with braided hair or gold or pearls or expensive clothes.*

The word *modest* here is the Greek word *kosmios*, which means "of good behavior, decorum, decent, modest." The opposite is the word *kosmikos*, which means "corrupt" or "worldly."

What do you think it means *not* to dress like the world?

....

....

What are some examples of dressing like the world?

....

....

Lord, it's clear in Your Word that You want us to be set apart. Help me remember this when I choose what I will wear each day. In Jesus' name, amen.

Day Three
Read Daniel 1:8.

*But Daniel resolved not to defile himself with the royal food and
wine, and he asked the chief official for permission not to defile
himself this way.*

When I looked at this verse in my Bible, I noticed I had pre-
viously scribbled the words "my covenant" in the margin. In the
New International Version, the word used for Daniel's decision to
abstain from the king's table is "resolved" while the King James
Version reads "purposed." In the Hebrew text the word is *suwm*
(pronounced *soom*), and it means "to commit or determine." But
one thing each of these words has in common is that they are all
past tense. Daniel made up his mind to stand firm before he knew
how the news would be taken!

This is why it is so important to make the decision *now* to avoid
immodesty—before next season's trends come out, before you go
shopping, before the rest of your life.

What are your thoughts about being resolved in your decisions about
dressing before situations arise that might tempt you to compromise
your beliefs? What situations might arise that could cause you to waver
in your resolve?

Girlfriend, know that I have been on both sides of this issue. I have been both stubborn and sensitive, immovable and impressionable. You are in my prayers.

Lord Jesus, it's not easy to make a commitment or a covenant not knowing what opposition it may bring, but I pray for courage to be obedient to Your Word. In Jesus' name, amen.

Day Four
Read Proverbs 25:26.

> *Like a muddied spring or a polluted well*
> *is a righteous man who gives way to the wicked.*

Daniel purposed in his heart not to "defile" himself. This word means literally "pollute or stain."

What do you think of when you hear the word *pollute*?

....

....

When I think of something being polluted, I imagine the contaminants and actions (pollutions and polluting) that caused it. We know once an environment, such as a body of water or a city, becomes polluted it can take many years to clean it up. The same can be true with our reputations. Whether we like it or not, what we wear can have an effect on our reputations. How can our reputations affect our testimony or how we live out our Christian faith in public?

....

....

....

....

Do you think people pay more attention to what we say or what we do? Why?

....

....

....

....

Lord, help me remember my actions often speak louder than my words. In Jesus' name, amen.

Day Five
Read Jeremiah 2:22.

> *"Although you wash yourself with soda*
> *and use an abundance of soap,*
> *the stain of your guilt is still before me,"*
> *declares the Sovereign LORD.*

The prophet Jeremiah wrote these words to the Hebrews who were once obedient to and loved God, but then turned away. God defines their sin and guilt as a stain. Going back to our word study of Daniel 1:8, and Daniel's decision not to defile or stain himself, what do you think of when you hear the word *stain*?

....

....

The word *stain* makes me think of laundry and my favorite clothes being ruined by stains. When something is stained, it's permanent; otherwise, it would just be dirty. Sin stains our lives in the same way. Write Isaiah 1:18:

....

....

Isn't that one of the greatest verses ever? God tells us although our sins are as scarlet they will be white as snow. That's a permanent fix for what *was* a permanent problem. He knows we're dirty. He knows we're stained. And He knew He was the only One who could wash us white as snow! Through His death and resurrection we can be forgiven of every sin that has stained us, even the little stains. Ponder this: if you had a beautiful white gown with a small, dark red stain on the back where your rear is, would you be comfortable wearing it? Why or why not?

....

....

No way would I wear it, because I know what it looks like! Some people believe they're okay, because they're not *big stain* sinners. As we can see from the dress analogy, even the small stains ruin what could have been beautiful. God sees us the same way. No matter how big or small, we're all still sinners and in need of a Savior.

Lord, Your Word teaches us that the sins we consider small still defile us. Help us see them through Your eyes—as pollutants and stains in need of a cleansing that only You can do. In Jesus' name, amen.

Chapter Four: Fashioned for Faithfulness

Day One

Read the following verses:

> A wife of noble character is her husband's crown,
> but a disgraceful wife is like decay in his bones.
>
> —Proverbs 12:4

> A wife of noble character who can find?
> She is worth far more than rubies.
>
> —Proverbs 31:10

> And now, my daughter, don't be afraid. I will do for you all you
> ask. All my fellow townsmen know that you are a woman of noble
> character.
>
> —Ruth 3:11

These verses speak of a woman with what attribute? What does this
characteristic mean to you?

....

....

These three verses all use the same Hebrew word that means "virtuous." *Webster's Dictionary* defines *virtuous* as "moral excellence." It's not mediocre morality; it's not kind-of-sort-of-most-times morality; it's morality at its highest—a level of excellence. Do you think it's important for a woman of God to have this kind of excellence? Do you think we should also aspire for our wardrobes to be moral and excellent? If so, why and how?

....

....

Lord, this is obviously a virtue You consider important. Help us guard it with the same level of importance. In Jesus' name, amen.

Day Two

Read the following verses from Proverbs 31:

She makes coverings for her bed;
she is clothed in fine linen and purple. (v. 22)

She is clothed with strength and dignity;
she can laugh at the days to come. (v. 25)

We learned in this chapter just how God says we should clothe
ourselves. In these verses of Proverbs, what are the four words used to
describe how this woman is clothed? What do those words mean?

....

....

....

....

Two of these words reference her physical appearance, while the
other two reference her heart's appearance. Do you think more people
notice your physical wardrobe or the state and nature of your inner
beauty? Why?

....

....

Oh Lord, help us always put more time and effort into our hearts' appearance than the time we spend in front of a mirror. In Jesus' name, amen.

Day Three

Read Proverbs 31:30.

> *Charm is deceptive, and beauty is fleeting;*
>   *but a woman who fears the LORD is to be praised.*

What does "beauty is fleeting" mean?

....

....

How do people rely on their physical beauty?

....

....

On what or whom does God want us to rely? Why?

....

....

Lord, sometimes it's easier to emphasize our beauty with makeup and wardrobe choices. Help us understand that the beauty You see is *not* the beauty that fades. In Jesus' name, amen.

Day Four

Reread Proverbs 31:30.

> *Charm is deceptive, and beauty is fleeting;*
> *but a woman who fears the LORD is to be praised.*

The word *fear* in this verse means "reverence." It is another word for respect. Specifically, how can we respect God and His Word?

....

....

....

If God's Word is clear about immodesty and the devastation it can cause a brother, can we still choose to dress immodestly yet claim to have reverential respect toward God and His perfect Word? Why or why not?

....

....

....

What does this verse say will happen if a woman fears the Lord?

....

....

....

The word *praised* in this verse is a Hebrew word that means "to shine." Have you ever seen a woman who so loves the Lord she seems to shine? I know a woman like this. Her name is Terri, and her joy for Jesus is the most alluring part of her beauty. We all aspire to physical beauty. Now let's aspire to really *shine*!

Lord, You are God. Your desire is for us to shine from the inside out. Help us show respect for You and Your perfect Word. In Jesus' name, amen.

Day Five
Read Ephesians 2:10.

For we are God's workmanship, created in Christ Jesus to do good works, which God prepared in advance for us to do.

The Greek word for "workmanship" is a figurative word for "fabric." The idea is that God wove us like a beautiful piece of tapestry. To weave an intricate fabric like this takes time and a great deal of attention. I've always found it interesting that the front is perfect and lovely while the back is tangled and ugly. I think this is sometimes how we see ourselves—like the back of a tapestry. I know there was a time when I did!

In my middle school years, I was tall, thin, and gangly. All the girls were filling out except me—I looked like a skinny boy with puffy hair! I had braces and bad skin. I never dated a popular boy and definitely was not part of the in-crowd. In fact, three older and bigger girls constantly harassed me and threatened to beat me up . . . for no reason. I used to find different routes to my classes so I wouldn't run into one of them. I was uncomfortable in my skin but always put on a happy face so no one would know. Even though I felt unraveled and ugly, God saw me for what was most beautiful.

If you struggle in this same area, please know God created you and He absolutely loves and *adores* you. Take Him at His word. You are wonderfully designed and created by the God of the universe who wants to spend eternity with lovely, *more beautiful you!*

Your thoughts:

....

....

....

....

....

....

....

....

....

....

Lord, sometimes it's so easy to see ourselves as the back of a tapestry—tangled and ugly. We get discouraged when our skin or hair isn't just right, or when we're convinced that we don't measure up to society's standards. Change me, Lord. Help me know that I am a beautiful creation. Allow my heart and mind to accept my body as Your workmanship and Your masterpiece! In Jesus' name, amen.

Chapter Five: Fashioned to Be Feminine

Day One
Read 1 Corinthians 3:16–17.

> *Don't you know that you yourselves are God's temple and that God's Spirit lives in you? If anyone destroys God's temple, God will destroy him; for God's temple is sacred, and you are that temple.*

This passage is written to believers in Jesus Christ. And Paul (the author) is emphatic about the importance of our bodies as the dwelling place of God. How does this knowledge make you feel?

....

....

....

In verse 17 Paul is very clear that God's temple—our bodies—is *sacred*. Using a dictionary, define *sacred*.

....

....

....

Do you treat your body as sacred, as God's temple? Explain:

....

....

....

Lord, teach me to regard and treat my body as Your temple, a sacred dwelling place. In Jesus' name, amen.

Day Two
Read 1 Corinthians 6:19–20.

> *Do you not know that your body is a temple of the Holy Spirit,*
> *who is in you, whom you have received from God? You are not*
> *your own; you were bought at a price. Therefore honor God with*
> *your body.*

Some people assume their bodies belong to themselves, but this passage clearly explains our bodies belong to the Lord. In fact, we can't take another breath or make our hearts beat another beat if God doesn't allow us to. Verse 20 says we are to "honor God" with our bodies. What are some ways we can do this?

....

....

....

Are you doing these things? If not, why?

....

....

....

Father, help me honor You with my body, in how I dress it, feed it, exercise it, and move it. In Jesus' name, amen.

Day Three
Read 1 Corinthians 10:31.

> *So whether you eat or drink or whatever you do, do it all for the glory of God.*

What areas of our lives does this passage refer to? Are there areas in your life in which you struggle with glorifying God?

....

....

How can you glorify God with your body today?

....

....

Can you make a commitment to always strive to honor God with your body?

....

God, if we're honest, it's much easier to let You be Lord of our lives when we need Your help than to be Lord of our bodies day to day, but that's what You seek from us . . . *everything.* Help us give You all we have, including—and especially—our temples. In Jesus' name, amen.

Day Four

Read Psalm 33:22.

> *May your unfailing love rest upon us, O LORD,*
> *even as we put our hope in you.*

God loves us as we are. Whether fat, skinny, short, or tall, He loves us with an *unfailing* love. But so often we put our hopes into the image we see—or would like to see—in the mirror.

He loves us as we are, because He created us as we are. Unfortunately, society and media bombard us with images that cause us to question His creation. His voice is the only one that matters, and He says we are beautiful (Song of Solomon 4:1).

List some of your favorite attributes about yourself—physical, emotional, and mental:

....

....

....

....

....

....

....

Lord, thank You for loving me as I am with a love that is unfailing. I cannot earn Your love, for You love me because You created me and I am Yours. Help me keep that perspective when I feel overwhelmed by secular society. Help me see the worth of my internal beauty instead of focusing so much on what is external. In Jesus' name, amen.

Day Five

Read 1 Corinthians 12:18, 22–23.

> *But in fact God has arranged the parts in the body, every one of them, just as he wanted them to be. . . . On the contrary, those parts of the body that seem to be weaker are indispensable, and the parts that we think are less honorable we treat with special honor. And the parts that are unpresentable are treated with special modesty.*

This passage refers to the parts of the body of believers. The apostle Paul is saying we, as Christians, are all a part of a bigger picture, the body of Christ. We all have different qualities, and He designed us with that in mind. But it is also teaches us that God wants us to see that our physical bodies are also arranged as He wants them to be. Dr. Charles Ryrie suggests in his commentary on verse 23 the "parts that are unpresentable are treated with special honor" refers to clothing.[1]

Besides clothing, what are some other ways we can treat our bodies with "special honor"?

. . . .

. . . .

. . . .

Dear Lord, help me see that my body is a temple—Your temple—and it belongs solely to You. You care about how I treat it, care for it, and present it. Teach me to be faithful, Lord. In Jesus' name, amen.

Your thoughts:

....

....

....

....

....

....

Chapter Six: Fashioned for a Frame

Day One
Read Psalm 139:1–3, 13–16, 23–24.

> O LORD, you have searched me
>> and you know me.
> You know when I sit and when I rise;
>> you perceive my thoughts from afar.
> You discern my going out and my lying down;
>> you are familiar with all my ways. . . .
>
> For you created my inmost being;
>> you knit me together in my mother's womb.
> I praise you because I am fearfully and wonderfully made;
>> your works are wonderful,
>> I know that full well.
> My frame was not hidden from you
>> when I was made in the secret place.
> When I was woven together in the depths of the earth,
>> your eyes saw my unformed body.
> All the days ordained for me
>> were written in your book
>> before one of them came to be. . . .
>
> Search me, O God, and know my heart;
>> test me and know my anxious thoughts.
> See if there is any offensive way in me,
>> and lead me in the way everlasting.

This is a humble passage about the handiwork and knowledge of God, but it closes in verses 23 and 24 with issues of anxiety and trust. In what ways do you find yourself anxious about your body?

....

....

....

....

Lord, help me celebrate my body—not just tolerate it—for it is wonderfully made! In Jesus' name, amen.

Day Two

Read Psalm 45:11.

> *The king is enthralled by your beauty;*
> *honor him, for he is your lord.*

Ultimately, "the king" refers to Jesus Christ, the King of kings. And because we are His daughters, we are princesses!

Rewrite the verse to include your name:

....

....

What are some of the responsibilities you have as a representative and daughter of the King?

....

....

....

Oh Lord, help me to represent You well in all I do. In Jesus' name, amen.

Day Three

Read Ephesians 4:14; 5:6.

> *Then we will no longer be infants, tossed back and forth by the waves, and blown here and there by every wind of teaching and by the cunning and craftiness of men in their deceitful scheming. . . . Let no one deceive you with empty words, for because of such things God's wrath comes on those who are disobedient.*

Who do you think the Bible is referring to as cunning, crafty men?

....

....

Can you find the parallel with these passages and the influence the media has on our view of ourselves, and if so, what is it?

....

....

....

According to the beginning of Ephesians 4:14, what impact does their "deceitful scheming" have on us?

....

....

....

....

Lord, if we're not careful, we will become insecure and tossed back and forth simply by the suggestions and opinions of others. Thank You for verse 14, which offers us hope that we will *no longer* have to believe the lies. Let today be the day I take You at Your word! In Jesus' name, amen.

Day Four

Read Ephesians 4:17–19.

> *So I tell you this, and insist on it in the Lord, that you must no longer live as the Gentiles do, in the futility of their thinking. They are darkened in their understanding and separated from the life of God because of the ignorance that is in them due to the hardening of their hearts. Having lost all sensitivity, they have given themselves over to sensuality so as to indulge in every kind of impurity, with a continual lust for more.*

Paul used the term *Gentiles* as another word for unbelievers. What characteristics did he use to describe them?

....

....

....

These are traits that prove their lack of morals and membership in the body of Christ. For me, it is a convicting list. How do you measure up to it?

....

....

....

....

....

What pattern is mentioned at the end of verse 19?

....

....

How does this manifest itself in fashion today?

....

....

....

Father, You have taught us to be set apart from the world. Convict me of the areas in my life that need to come under Your authority, and give me the boldness and willpower to change. In Jesus' name, amen.

Day Five

Read Ephesians 4:20–24.

> *You, however, did not come to know Christ that way. Surely you heard of him and were taught in him in accordance with the truth that is in Jesus. You were taught, with regard to your former way of life, to put off your old self, which is being corrupted by its deceitful desires; to be made new in the attitude of your minds; and to put on the new self, created to be like God in true righteousness and holiness.*

What hope is found in these verses?

....

....

....

....

Would you describe this as an instruction or a promise or both? Explain:

....

....

....

Does this process begin in our emotions or in our minds? Is it a conscious decision?

. . . .

. . . .

In her simulcast *So Long Insecurity,* Beth Moore states that we must make a choice to be secure even before we feel secure. It begins in the mind. Live in accordance with that truth *and then* it will collide with our emotions. Have you had an experience like that?

. . . .

. . . .

. . . .

God, I want to make the deliberate decision to put off the old self and put on the new self, one that is created to be like Christ in true righteousness and holiness. Help me live it out beginning right now. In Jesus' name, amen.

Chapter Seven: Fashioned to Bear Fruit

Day One
Read Galatians 5:16–17, 24.

> *So I say, live by the Spirit, and you will not gratify the desires of*
> *the sinful nature. For the sinful nature desires what is contrary*
> *to the Spirit, and the Spirit what is contrary to the sinful nature.*
> *They are in conflict with each other, so that you do not do what*
> *you want. . . . Those who belong to Christ Jesus have crucified the*
> *sinful nature with its passions and desires.*

The Bible teaches that we are born sinners. I noticed this with both my
children, Jack and Jude. Though they are precious and entertaining,
they are born with the same sinful desires the rest of us are born with.
The other night over dinner, my husband and I recalled that two of the
first words they learned to speak were "No!" and "Mine!" In Christ,
we must crucify these sinful desires and replace them with the fruits of
the Spirit. What "passions and desires" of the sinful nature need to be
crucified in your life? And what fruits should replace them?

Crucify: Replace with Spiritual Fruit:

....

....

....

....

....

....

....

Lord, help us demonstrate Your work in us through the fruits of the Spirit. In Jesus' name, amen.

Day Two

Read Galatians 5:19–20.

> *The acts of the sinful nature are obvious: sexual immorality,*
> *impurity and debauchery; idolatry and witchcraft; hatred, dis-*
> *cord, jealousy.*

Define the acts of the sinful nature in verses 19 and 20:

1. Sexual immorality:

....

....

2. Impurity and debauchery:

....

....

3. Idolatry and witchcraft:

....

....

4. Hatred:

....

....

5. Discord:

....

....

6. Jealousy:

....

....

Can you think of any areas in your life where even a hint of these is present? Just like the fruits of the Spirit confirm that we are walking with God, the acts of the sinful nature confirm that we are falling short of His best.

Lord, You know we have fallen short in all these ways, but we are thankful for Your forgiveness and restoration. Help us surrender afresh to the work You want to do in our lives! In Jesus' name, amen.

Day Three

Read Galatians 5:20–21.

> . . . *fits of rage, selfish ambition, dissensions, factions and envy; drunkenness, orgies, and the like.*

List and define the acts of the sinful nature in verses 20 and 21:

1. Fits of rage:

....

....

2. Selfish ambition:

....

....

3. Dissentions:

....

....

4. Factions and envy:

....

....

5. Drunkenness:

....

....

6. Orgies and the like:

....

....

List the categories immodesty falls under in the full list of the sinful nature, and then describe how it fits within that category:

1. ....

....

2. ....

....

3. ....

....

4. ....

....

5. ....

....

Think of these scenarios if you need help: showing cleavage, wearing miniskirts, spending too much time in front of the mirror, wearing T-shirts with vampire endorsements, being angry at your parents about your clothing limitations, wanting what another girl is wearing, wearing trends without regard for your Christian brothers, operating in cliques because of fashion.

The Bible covers a lot of ground, and to understand its depth, sometimes we have to filter everything we want to do through an exhaustive list like this. If the thing we want to do doesn't pass this biblical litmus test, it is best to avoid it.

Lord, this is a long list and can be overwhelming at any stage of our Christian lives. Help us to be sensitive to the things You call sin. In Jesus' name, amen.

Day Four

Read Galatians 6:7–8.

> *Do not be deceived: God cannot be mocked. A man reaps what he sows. The one who sows to please his sinful nature, from that nature will reap destruction; the one who sows to please the Spirit, from the Spirit will reap eternal life.*

Write out these verses in your own words:

....

....

These verses deal with the effects of our actions. Although there are different consequences depending on the offense, sin is sin. And no sin is greater than another—they all held Jesus on the cross. Nevertheless, we are left with a choice: to reap the sinful nature of our flesh or to walk according to the Spirit.

What might we reap if we choose immodesty?

....

....

Lord, it's obvious that many of the decisions we make will either reap the sinful nature born in us or the fruits of the Spirit that You bore in us at salvation. Help us not to make excuses for our sins, but to confess them and turn from them. Grow a harvest of spiritual fruit in our lives! In Jesus' name, amen.

Day Five

Read Galatians 6:9.

> *Let us not become weary in doing good, for at the proper time we*
> *will reap a harvest if we do not give up.*

It can be an overwhelming task to live according to the Spirit instead of the flesh. In fact, without God, we cannot. Paul encourages believers on many occasions not to give up. Is there something in your life right now that God seems to have put His finger on? If so, what is it?

....

....

Girlfriend, let me encourage you to press on, and let the Holy One of heaven move through you to accomplish it!

Lord, I am convinced that You brought _____ to my mind because You want to replace it with spiritual fruit. I surrender it now. In Jesus' name, amen.

Chapter Eight: Fashioned to Follow Through

Day One
Read Acts 17:11.

> *Now the Bereans were of more noble character than the Thessalonians, for they received the message with great eagerness and examined the Scriptures every day to see if what Paul said was true.*

How were the Bereans different from the Thessalonians?

....

....

....

I don't want you to just take me at my word; I want you to take God at His. I have searched the Scriptures and given you insight on the subject of modesty. But ultimately, it is up to you to search the Bible—even the same Scriptures that we have covered—and ask God to reveal truth to you. Only be careful to have an open heart, willing to hear, listen, and obey. You will be in my prayers as you seek the final authority on modesty—God.

Father, Your love for Your daughters is unmatched! You want us to know Your truths and follow through in obedience. Teach us to search Your word and to accept Your authority in every situation. We are desolate without Your wisdom! In Jesus' name, amen.

Day Two

Read Philippians 3:13–15.

> *Brothers, I do not consider myself yet to have taken hold of it. But one thing I do: Forgetting what is behind and straining toward what is ahead, I press on toward the goal to win the prize for which God has called me heavenward in Christ Jesus. All of us who are mature should take such a view of things. And if on some point you think differently, that too God will make clear to you.*

What do you think it means when it says we "should take such a view of [these] things"?

. . . .

. . . .

I'm glad that Paul included the last sentence of verse 15. Write it here:

. . . .

. . . .

Dr. Charles Ryrie notes that Paul means, "in effect, 'if you don't agree, God will give you light on the subject.'"[2] Right now, how do you feel about the issue of modesty as we have studied it?

. . . .

. . . .

....

....

Lord, please continue to shed light on the subject of modesty for me and help me understand Your "view of things." In Jesus' name, amen.

Day Three
Read James 1:5.

> *If any of you lacks wisdom, he should ask God, who gives gener-*
> *ously to all without finding fault, and it will be given to him.*

How can this passage resolve any questions we might still have about how we dress?

....

....

What Scripture has spoken the most directly to you about how God feels about the issue of modesty?

....

....

God, without Your wisdom, I cannot know Your will for my life or how to make godly decisions. Please grant me wisdom to know how I should dress so my wardrobe choices will honor You. In Jesus' name, amen.

Day Four

Read James 1:6–8.

> *But when he asks, he must believe and not doubt, because he who doubts is like a wave of the sea, blown and tossed by the wind. That man should not think he will receive anything from the Lord; he is a double-minded man, unstable in all he does.*

Write out these verses, changing the "he" to "she" and the "man" to "woman."

....

....

....

....

....

How important would you say that it is for us to be willing to obey God, even before we understand His will on a subject?

....

Explain:

....

....

....

....

God wants our hearts. Period. He doesn't want us to fish around for what we *want* His Word to say; He wants us to take Him at His Word, believe it, and live by it.

Lord, I know Your Word is true, and I want Your imparted wisdom. Help me to live by faith in obedience to what Your Word says, even when it's hard. In Jesus' name, amen.

Day Five
Read James 4:17.

Anyone, then, who knows the good he ought to do and doesn't do it, sins.

This is probably the hardest verse in Scripture for me to digest, but I cannot deny it. Describe your thoughts or apprehensions about it:

....

....

....

....

God, I want to walk closely with You and know Your heart. My stubbornness separates me from You and prevents me from hearing Your voice. Convict me when I am out of Your will, and give me the courage to obey Your Word. I want to know "the good I ought to do" and do it! In Jesus' name, amen.

Chapter Nine: Fashioned Forever

If you just received Jesus as your Savior or did so a long time ago, the following verses provide a foundation for your faith in Christ:

Day One: A New Creation

Read 2 Corinthians 5:17.

> *Therefore, if anyone is in Christ, he is a new creation; the old has gone, the new has come!*

This verse reminds me of the image of a caterpillar turning into a butterfly. The old is gone—the butterfly can never become a caterpillar again—it is a new creation! Though it is the same living creature, it is now different. That is what happens to us when we are born again. If you are willing, there will be things in your life that will change as a result of your new identity. And just like a butterfly, it is beautiful!

What are some things in your life you think God wants to change?

....

....

....

Bible commentator Albert Barnes states about salvation:

There is a change so deep, so clear, so entire, and so abiding, that it is proper to say, here is a new creation of God—a work of the divine power as decided and as glorious as when God created all things out of nothing. There is no other moral change that takes place on earth so deep, and radical, and thorough as the change at conversion. And there is no other where there is so much propriety in ascribing it to the mighty power of God.[3]

Thank You, Lord, for making me a new creation—changed from the inside out—a change that only You can make! Help me grow as a new creation to become the woman of God You want me to be! In Jesus' name, amen.

Day Two: Security

Read the following verses:

> *I give them eternal life, and they shall never perish; no one can snatch them out of my hand.*
>
> —John 10:28

> *I write these things to you who believe in the name of the Son of God so that you may know that you have eternal life.*
>
> —1 John 5:13

According to John 10:28, no one can snatch us from God's hand. What does that truth mean to you?

....

....

....

These two verses offer us the security of our salvation. In other words, as 1 John suggests, we have a "know so" salvation, not a "think so" salvation.

Oh Lord, what wonderful news! Thank You that I am secure in Your grip and no one—not even Satan—nor any sin I commit can cause me to lose my salvation! The change You made in me is deep and irreversible! I praise You for making me Yours! In Jesus' name, amen.

Day Three: The Word
Read Psalm 119:11, 105.

> *I have hidden your word in my heart*
> *that I might not sin against you. . . .*
> *Your word is a lamp to my feet*
> *and a light for my path.*

These verses speak of the importance of reading and knowing God's written Word, the Bible. Taking time daily to read God's Word is like food for the soul—it has to have it to sustain spiritual muscles. Some days I read a psalm and a proverb. Other days I choose a book like Ephesians and read a couple of chapters a day, asking God to speak to me through His Word. Also, there are different translations that help us to understand Scripture better. Some easy-to-understand ones are the New International Version, *The Message*, or my favorite, the New Living Translation.

Decide how you will proceed with a daily quiet time with the Lord. There is no right or wrong method. List your ideas:

....

....

....

Father, I pray that You'll help me understand the Bible as I read it. Please give me a hunger for knowing You better through Your Word. In Jesus' name, amen.

Day Four: Prayer

Read the following verses:

Evening, morning and noon
I cry out in distress, and he hears my voice.

—Psalm 55:17

Be joyful in hope, patient in affliction, faithful in prayer.

—Romans 12:12

Devote yourselves to prayer, being watchful and thankful.

—Colossians 4:2

Salvation is a relationship, and no relationship can be strong without communication. Prayer is the vehicle God uses to allow us to communicate with Him, and, if we're quiet, we can hear His still, small voice speaking to us through His Word. It's amazing that we have the privilege of communicating directly with the Creator of the universe!

Make a habit of writing down prayer requests and the answers that come. It's encouraging to look back on all that God has done in our lives. Here is a template to get you started:

Date/Request: **Date/Answer:**

....

....

....

....

....

....

....

....

....

....

Thank You, Lord, that I don't have to have instructions on how to talk to You. I can talk to You as I would talk to a best friend and share my deepest struggles, fears, and joys. I can talk to You alone in my bed, driving down the highway . . . anywhere—even in the bathroom! You desire to hear from me. Create that same desire in me to spend time with You in prayer every day. In Jesus' name, amen.

Day Five: Sanctification
Read Matthew 5:8.

> *Blessed are the pure in heart,*
> *for they will see God.*

I love this verse. "The pure in heart." It speaks of heaven, certainly—that we will actually be in the presence of God someday. But it also teaches us that being pure in heart is a daily opportunity to experience God. No guy, bank account, status, or wardrobe can satisfy—only the immeasurable greatness of the King of kings!

If we seek to be pure in heart in everything that we do, God will transform us by the renewing of our minds. When we do, we see our former selfish ambitions pass away. It's what the Bible refers to as *sanctification*—the process of Christian growth.

In Isaiah 61:3, we read of becoming mighty "oaks of righteousness." An oak tree doesn't become full-grown overnight. It first begins as an acorn that falls to the ground and dies. The old, hard shell of the acorn is no longer necessary, because the fragile shoot now makes its home in the soft earth. Its roots begin to grow deep into the soil as it grows stronger. Even though it's small, it is no less an oak tree than the towering full-grown oaks. Over time, it will endure even the greatest storms, provide shelter and food for small animals, and produce more trees from its fruit.

I picture the hard outer shell of the acorn as our life before Christ. When we're born again, we leave our sinful ways and turn to Christ—our new master. Our life is *in* Him, like the baby tree's life is *in* the soil. We may stumble and fall as baby Christians because it's a new way of life for us. Just because we are small, we are no less born again than one who's been saved for decades. Then, as we grow in sanctification—through daily prayer, Bible reading, and fellowship with other Christians—we become stronger, like the mighty oak. And as we grow, we can endure life's storms, provide comfort and encouragement for others, and produce fruit—the fruits of the Spirit.

Modesty is just one way we grow in sanctification. You may already be an oak of righteousness, or perhaps you're that little shoot trying for the first time to dig your roots in deep. Either way, I hope that through this in-depth study, you have seen the importance of modesty and the effect it has on our testimonies, the guys we try to impress, and our relationship and obedience to God. He changed me, and He can change you.

I pray that this will be the start of a great adventure in your relationship with God and that you will seek to know Him more. Just as I stated in the first chapter, modesty begins in the heart. If your heart is changed, you will see modesty as a growing fashion trend. Then we can show off our best side . . . our INSIDE!

Acknowledgments

My deepest appreciation to:

My friend and Savior, Jesus. Thank You for saving me and having patience with me. I am honored and humbled that You would allow me to share in Your great work.

MacKenzie Howard and the team at Thomas Nelson. Thank you for giving this no-name author a chance! Your tireless work and enthusiasm bless and encourage me.

Les Stobbe. You have been a true friend from the day we met. Thank you for your unwavering support! You believed in me when others passed. Thank you for reflecting Jesus in your leadership and representing us both beautifully.

Jessica, Eva, Julie, Bethany, and Vonda. You dethroned this self-proclaimed grammar queen! I am so grateful for your editing abilities. (My readers will be too!)

Shane and Bonnie Greene. Thank you for your steadfast friendship and photo expertise! I am deeply indebted to you both.

Seth, Tyler, Tommy, Cody, Hayden, Brandon, Tre', Chase, and Ty. This book would be incomplete without your candor and willingness to speak out. Thank you for your testimonies and love for Christ.

Dr. Ruffin Snow. Thank you for stretching me to uncover the truth about modesty. My message began with you.

My Friends for Christ Sunday school class and the group from Roan Mountain. Thank you for your prayers and encouragement and for standing with me as I tossed my stick—and my ambition—into the flames.

My friend and confidante, Terri Broome. Without you having taught me brokenness and surrender, this message would have been lost in my pride. You are an exemplary woman of God, and I love you.

Mom. Thank you for your encouragement and excitement as we watched God work another miracle. I love you and am grateful that I can count on you for anything.

Jack and Jude. People sometimes wonder why I would write a book for young women when I have boys. My answer is always "Because I have boys!" I pray that your eyes and hearts will forever be guarded and that you'll both be Job 31:1 men of God. You are so loved!

Daryl. I am blessed to have you as my husband. Thank you for honoring me as your object of affection and for looking away when others would ogle at provocatively dressed women. Thank you for believing in this cause and standing with me as I stepped out in obedience. Thank you for loving Jesus and representing Him in our family. I will love you forever.

Notes

Chapter One:

1. Greek and Hebrew translations of words are from James Strong, *Strong's Exhaustive Concordance of the Bible* (Peabody, MA: Hendrickson Publishers, 1988).

Chapter Two:

1. David Guzik, "2 Samuel 11: David's Adultery and Murder," EnduringWord.com, 2002, http://www.enduringword.com/commentaries/1011.htm.
2. Adam Clarke, "Clarke's Commentary: 2 Samuel 11," GodRules.net, 1831, http://www.godrules.net/library/clarke/clarke2sam11.htm.
3. Guzik, "2 Samuel 11: David's Adultery and Murder."
4. Dannah Gresh, *Secret Keeper* (Chicago: Moody Publishers, 2005), 54.
5. Lillian Hellman, "I Cannot and Will Not Cut My Conscience to Fit This Year's Fashions," History Matters, May 21, 1952, http://historymatters.gmu.edu/d/6454.

Chapter Three:

1. Matthew Henry, "Daniel 1: Matthew Henry's Concise Commentary on the Bible," Biblos.com, 2004, http://mhc.biblecommenter.com/daniel/1.htm.

Chapter Four:

1. Jonny Diaz, "More Beautiful You," JonnyDiaz.com, March 10, 2009, http://www.jonnydiaz.com/?p=77.

Chapter Five:

1. "Did You Know," *Anorexia Nervosa Treatment*, 2010, http://www .anorexia-nervosa-treatment.net/did-you-know.php.

2. M. G. Lord, *Forever Barbie: The Unauthorized Biography of a Real Doll* (New York: William Morrow and Company, Inc., 1994).

Chapter Seven:

1. St. Francis of Assisi (Founder of the Franciscan order, 1181– 1226), ThinkExist.com, 2010, http://thinkexist.com/quotation/ preach_the_gospel_at_all_times_and_when_necessary/219332. html.

Chapter Eight:

1. Anonymous, "The Sin of Bathsheba: An Appeal to Christian Women by a Brother in Christ," DocStoc.com, http://www .docstoc.com/docs/33207490/The-Sin-of-Bathsheba.

2. Nancy Leigh DeMoss, "Mixed Messages," ReviveOurHearts. com, May 31, 2005, http://www.reviveourhearts.com/radio/ roh/today.php?pid=977.

3. Coco Chanel (French Fashion designer who ruled over Parisian haute couture for almost six decades, 1883–1971), ThinkExist .com, 2010, http://thinkexist.com/quotation/a-girl-shuld-be- two-things-classy-and/348233.html.

Conclusion:

1. Oswald Chambers, "The Habit of Keeping a Clear Conscience," MyUtmost.org, May 13 devotional, http://utmost.org/?s= the+habit+of+good+conscience&x=0&y=0.

Fashioned by Faith 45-Day Personal Quiet Time Diary

1. Charles C. Ryrie, *The Ryrie Study Bible, New International Version* (Chicago: Moody Press, 1986).
2. Ibid.
3. Albert Barnes, *Notes on the New Testament*, Kregel Classics, 8th ed., June 30, 1962, 854, http://bible.cc/2_corinthians/5-17.htm.

Looking for more?

Be sure to check out Rachel Lee Carter online

www.modelingchrist.com

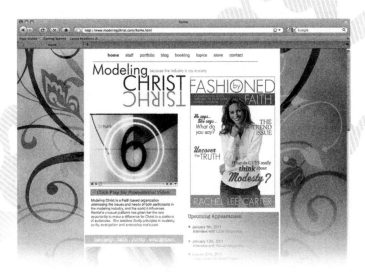

It's a great resource for all things Rachel!

» Blog
» Photos
» Speaking schedule

 Facebook: RachelLeeCarter

Twitter: @RachelLeeCarter

Meet the fabulous Izzy Baxter

Izzy Baxter has big plans- pop star plans!

Presented like a daily blog, set up like a devotional, and read like a novel—this book will be an instant hit with tween girls. This cutting edge new product will meet girls where they are, and girls will love following Izzy on her incredible adventure. Plus, they'll get daily spiritual food to equip them on their own incredible adventure with God.

AVAILABLE AT BOOKSTORES EVERYWHERE
978-1-4003-1654-0 | 978-1-4003-1737-0 (ebook)

Be sure to follow Izzy's adventures on her site at:
www.izzypopstarplan.com

TWITTER: @IzzyBaxter
FACEBOOK: Izzy's Pop Star Plan

A Division of Thomas Nelson Publishers

www.tommynelson.com

If God wanted April Grace to be kind to her neighbors, He should have made them nicer!

Growing up in the country is never easy, but it sure is funny—especially if you happen to have a sister obsessed with being glamorous, a grandma just discovering make-up, hippie friends who never shower, and brand new neighbors from the city who test everyone's patience. From disastrous dye jobs to forced apologies and elderly date tagalongs, you'll laugh 'til you cry as you read the *Confessions of April Grace*!

Available at bookstores everywhere | ISBN: 978-1-4003-1722-6

A Division of Thomas Nelson Publishers

www.tommynelson.com
Facebook: TommyNelsonKids   Twitter:@TommyNelson

Some strange things are happening in sleepy Middlefield…

Book #1	Book #2	Book # 3
978-1-4003-1593-2	978-1-4003-1620-5	978-1-4003-1719-6
978-1-4185-6031-7 e-book	978-1-4003-1734-9 e-book	

Don't miss a minute of the adventure in the
new Mysteries of Middlefield series by Kathleen Fuller

Available at bookstores everywhere

A Division of Thomas Nelson Publishers

www.tommynelson.com

Facebook: TommyNelsonKids   Twitter:@TommyNelson